In Praise of Coach Brey

"When I think about Coach Brey, I think of somebody who is a very smooth guy who gives a lot of trust and confidence to his players. He definitely gave me a lot of opportunities to show who I am on and off the court. He gave me an opportunity to play my freshman year, and it was kind of all she wrote after that. Thank you for teaching me to always have calm feet on the perimeter. And, also, thank you for spending time in the locker room with me when we both got our flagrant fouls."

—Bonzie Colson
Notre Dame player, 2014–18

"I'm a better coach, I'm a better teacher, I'm a better educator because of my opportunity of playing and working for him. I think he pushed me. He knew areas where I needed to improve. As a senior point guard, I was an extension of him on the floor. So we really connected."

—Martin Ingelsby
University of Delaware head coach
Former Notre Dame player and assistant coach

"Mike and I have grown up with the same background, going to DeMatha High School. The ability to touch these young men's lives means more than the number of championships we've won, and I think that is going to be his legacy more than anything."

—Rod Balanis
Notre Dame associate head coach

"Each guy that comes to his program is like his child, like his son. He takes that to heart. He instills a lot of trust, and for him to bring guys back to coach that played for him here means a lot for this culture. We're a representation of what he's kind of built here over the last 20 years."

—Ryan Ayers
Notre Dame assistant coach
Former Notre Dame player

"It's funny how time flies. I was here when he got his first win. He had a little bit more hair. But it's fun to be back—to be part of the first one and now to be here when he breaks the record."

—Ryan Humphrey
Notre Dame assistant coach
Former Notre Dame player

"His biggest strength as a coach is belief in his players. He instills a confidence because of his belief and the freedom he gives them. Other coaches would be yelling and screaming, trying to motivate that way. He would go, 'Guys, we're good, don't worry about it. We're going to do this and that, and this is what's going to happen.' He's almost prophetic at times when he does that."

—Torrian Jones
University of Delaware assistant coach
Former Notre Dame player

"I was here when the program wasn't great my freshman year, and then we started moving up my sophomore year. Coach Brey took it to the next level and he started this program on a journey that it hadn't seen in a while. It was a little bit tarnished when he got here. He cleaned it up, made it all sparkly and new."

—Harold Swanagan
Notre Dame director of basketball operations
Former Notre Dame player

"The words I would use to describe Coach Brey first and foremost are educator, the one he uses to describe himself. He's the son of parents who were teachers. He's always viewed coaching as an educational mission. Secondly, he is a psychologist of the first order. Mike's ability to understand in the context of a team how to motivate individuals, yet maintain the dynamic of the team, is a remarkable skill that reflects how attuned he is to the personalities of each individual. And then finally—passion. He's an extremely passionate person—passionate about the university, passionate about his job, passionate about life. And fortunately for Notre Dame, that passion comes out in very positive ways as the self-proclaimed 'loosest coach in America.' "   —*Jack Swarbrick*
Notre Dame athletic director

"The best thing about him is he really treats you like a man. He treats you with respect, and that's on and off the floor. He knows the game really well and he keeps it simple. He gives you a lot of freedom to play—and he trusts you. When you have a coach that instills that trust in you, that goes throughout the whole team, and then you start trusting everybody else. It's special to have, and he's created a culture here that kind of resembles his attitude and his approach to the game. He gave me a chance to come here and play. It wasn't easy at first. But I was lucky enough to develop a relationship with him through my four years here where we got pretty close, and we could talk about things that didn't even include basketball."   —*Matt Farrell*
Notre Dame player, 2014–18

Keeping It Loose

PATIENCE, PASSION,
AND
MY LIFE IN BASKETBALL

Mike Brey
with John Heisler

TRIUMPH
BOOKS

Library of Congress Cataloging-in-Publication Data
Names: Brey, Mike, author. | Heisler, John, author.
Title: Keeping it loose : patience, passion, and my life in basketball / Mike Brey with John Heisler.
Description: Chicago, Illinois : Triumph Books LLC, [2018]
Identifiers: LCCN 2018026821 | ISBN 9781629375977
Subjects: LCSH: Brey, Mike. | Basketball coaches—United States— Biography. | University of Notre Dame—Basketball—History.
Classification: LCC GV884.B74 A3 2018 | DDC 796.323092 [B] — dc23 LC record available at https://lccn.loc.gov/2018026821

This book is available in quantity at special discounts for your group or organization. For further information, contact:

Triumph Books LLC
814 North Franklin Street
Chicago, Illinois 60610
(312) 337-0747
www.triumphbooks.com

Printed in U.S.A.

ISBN: 978-1-62937-597-7

Design by Sue Knopf

To my parents, Paul and Betty,
the ultimate role models as educators

Contents

Foreword *by Jay Bilas* 11

Introduction 15

Chapter 1   From the Mock Turtle to the Open Collar . . . 21

Chapter 2   The Notre Dame Way 27

Chapter 3   The Chase to 400 37

Chapter 4   Growing Up on the Beltway 47

Chapter 5   Working for DeMatha's Master Mentor 61

Chapter 6   The Duke Years 69

Chapter 7   The Delaware Years 87

Chapter 8   Coming to Notre Dame, Finally 103

Chapter 9   The Early Years 121

Chapter 10   Players from the Early Years 143

Chapter 11   Feeling the Burn 169

Chapter 12   From the Big East to the ACC 183

Chapter 13   Triumph in the ACC   193

Chapter 14   From Harangody to Grant 209

Chapter 15   Connaughton, Colson, and Co. 231

Chapter 16   Coaches vs. Cancer and the NABC   263

              Afterword *by Morgan Wootten* 269

              Appendix I: Mike Brey's Wins
              Against Ranked Opponents 275

              Appendix II: Coaching Record 281

              Acknowledgments 285

Foreword

IN THE SUMMER OF 1987, I MET A YOUNG ASSISTANT COACH FROM DeMatha Catholic High School named Mike Brey. He was about to become the newest assistant coach on Mike Krzyzewski's staff at Duke. Mike and I met and were part of a group that had a casual dinner during a summer basketball camp on Duke's campus. Little did I know at that time, but Mike Brey would be one of the most profound influences on my life.

A few years later, I was named a graduate assistant on Coach K's staff at Duke, joining coaches Brey, Pete Gaudet, and Tommy Amaker. I spent the next three years sitting in Brey's office and watching him in practice and meetings, always learning from him. In addition to Brey's considerable basketball expertise, two things always stood out to me: his humility and his empathy.

After his playing career, he became a high school teacher and coach at DeMatha under the legendary Morgan Wootten. As a result of that experience (and his talent), Brey has always been keenly aware of the feelings and motivations of others. Armed with that empathy and humility, he has been able to use his extraordinary feel to reach people on a personal level and help them reach their full potential. When the pressure is on in the heat of battle—and tension and fear are in the air—he exhibits an incredible calm that is adopted by his players. And when things are too calm to the point of lethargy, he can raise the temperature with his unique blend of competitive fire and humor.

When he was the head coach at Delaware, I was fortunate enough to be assigned to call the championship game of the America East Conference. Brey's Blue Hens were a game away from an NCAA championship berth, which can lead to a tight, tension-filled atmosphere among players. He invited me into the Delaware locker room for a film session in preparation for the title game, and it was vintage Mike Brey. He showed important clips of the opponent and emphasized the key points for Delaware to win the championship. Then, as the film ended, Brey cautioned his team about something special the opponent may run at the end of a close game. As he set up this key championship point, he showed film from the movie *Hoosiers* and told his team to watch out for "the old picket fence" play, imploring his players not to "get caught watching the paint dry!" It was a closing bit of levity that had his players laughing and tension-free as they left the locker room for their final practice. It was a brilliant move.

But that's Mike Brey. When most coaches might be tight themselves and inject that tension into their teams, Brey has the feel to act off script to provide his players what they need to operate with a free mind and perform at the highest level. While Brey is fully in charge, he is humble enough to teach his players how to play and to trust them to execute without feeling micromanaged. He is a leader who empowers rather than controls.

Brey is as competitive as any person I have ever known, but he will never make another person feel uncomfortable based upon a negative outcome of a contest, no matter how much it hurt him to lose. He is never short with the media after a loss and is never unpleasant to be around after a loss. That, to me, is a true measure of empathy and humility. For Brey, it is not about how he feels; it is about how everyone around him feels.

Several years ago, one of his best players was dismissed from Notre Dame for an off-court error in judgment. Notre Dame has exacting standards and can be unforgiving when a student falls short of those exacting standards. Instead of leaving that player to find another place to play and simply wishing him well, as most coaches would do, Brey advocated patience and to do what it took to return to Notre Dame, even visiting him at his home with his Notre Dame jersey. Brey told him that he would someday re-enroll at Notre Dame, finish what he started, and have a storybook ending to his career in that very Irish uniform. And that is exactly what happened. Because Brey would not give up on his player, his player did not give up on Notre Dame. Brey's leadership turned what could have been a negative ending and a lifelong feeling of regret into an incredible positive for his player, for Notre Dame, and for Brey.

I am so grateful for the profound impact Brey has had upon my life and my career. He is a trusted friend and mentor, though I'm sure he would shrug his shoulders and suggest his influence was not a big deal. Then, he'd probably say, "Don't blame all that on me!" And we'd both have a great laugh. That's just who Mike Brey is. It is never about him.

I'm so glad that Brey has written this book. And I hope you will take from it the same things I have taken from him over the years: that Mike Brey is an incredibly smart, funny, empathetic, and humble person, who just happens to be one of the finest teachers and coaches in the game. I don't know a better person than Mike Brey.

—*Jay Bilas*
ESPN college basketball analyst

Introduction

THIS IS MY STORY. IT'S PART GROWING UP IN THE BALTIMORE/
Washington, D.C., area, part DeMatha Catholic High School, part
Duke University, part University of Delaware, and a lot of about
the University of Notre Dame.

Our vice president and athletic director at Notre Dame, Jack
Swarbrick, refers to our head coaches at Notre Dame as educator-
coaches. Based on the time our student-athletes spend with their
coaches, he strongly believes that we play as integral a role in their
college education as anyone else on campus. I love that. That's
always been my approach.

The games—wins and losses—are a part of it, and that's what
the fans see. But there's so much more to it behind the scenes, and
it's what being an educator is all about. When I was 13 or 14 years
old, coaching and teaching was something I wanted to do. Once
I got into high school, I can remember thinking about coaching
kids at camp with DeMatha High School coach Morgan Wootten.
It was something that was natural. My dad tried to talk me out of
coaching and teaching, but back then my biggest vision was to be
a high school coach.

I might have ended up a 30-year-career high school coach. Instead I stayed with Morgan, got the college bug, and then the Duke opportunity came about based on what Mike Krzyzewski needed. It was the perfect storm or I'd probably have been a high school coach in Montgomery County, Maryland, for 30 years.

Morgan's influence on me started when I was 10. I came to his day camp and was around the DeMatha players every day. Morgan was there teaching, coaching, and talking about basketball and life, so it was a dream to go to DeMatha. I played for him after going to his camp and then I coached with him. It was absolutely the best possible training.

After I graduated from George Washington, Morgan's greatest point was that I should join him if I wanted be a college coach. He said that—with all the players they had—everyone was going to be there recruiting so I would meet all kinds of people. And he was right on that. He also said that he wanted me to coach the junior varsity team for a couple of years because he thought I needed to have my own team. And he was really right about that one, too. You've got to make those decisions and sit in that seat. That really helped me when I became a head coach eight or nine years later.

The one phrase Mike K used when I interviewed for the Duke job? He said you're going to find out in college basketball that you have to compete every single day. That's the biggest thing I learned from him—the day-to-day intensity and preparation. He had that daily drive, and it was about competing every day.

My dad is a survivor of malignant melanoma. So my Coaches vs. Cancer involvement started back at Delaware. Then, when we came to Notre Dame, we wanted to stay with it, and now it's become our charity event. If I'm out in public, I'll get two questions about the team and then I'll get two comments about,

"Hey, Coach, I appreciate what you do with Coaches vs. Cancer because of what happened to my family." It really hits home with a lot of people.

We do what we do. It's a phrase we always use with our team. And when we do that, we're pretty consistent. And I'm really proud of that. We talk about doing even more, but you can't do anything until you have an identity.

When I got to Notre Dame, we had a 10-year void in terms of going to the NCAA Tournament, but you can't even talk about that unless you can make some headway in your league. We first had to become a consistent regular-season team in the Big East. We created a style of play and an identity—and now we're doing the same thing in the Atlantic Coast Conference.

I am so honored to be the coach at Notre Dame and I am so honored to be in the ACC. Based on my background, I'm very familiar with this league. There's still a little bit of newness about it for some people, and yet I think it's a great fit for our institution and I think more people on our campus appreciate that every day.

I love the kind of young man who is attracted to our place. That's why I love coaching at Notre Dame. Nothing's changed from the day they hired me. From Day One my goal was to do a good enough job where I could retire here. That's never really changed. I was at Duke when Mike K physically wore himself out and missed a season. So I think I've learned to pace myself through a year and through a season and understand when to shut it down.

Digger Phelps has been a good friend and a mentor. He was a little bit distant from the program when I got to Notre Dame, and my goal was to get him and some of our former players to feel good enough about our program that they'd want to come back and reconnect. It was my fourth year, and I said to him, "How about coming to a game next week?" And he said, "Al McGuire told me never to come back." But now he comes to most of our games. The one thing about Digger—when we talk privately and alone—is that he sat in this chair.

Be a confidence-giver. That's a theme I talk to our staff about. I think that's what I try to do. Coming from coaching and teaching at the high school level and having young people who aren't sure of themselves, you have to do that more on a daily basis with a 15-, 16-, 17-year-old. And nothing has changed. In those first few minutes after a game ends, as I'm walking to the tunnel, I'm trying to figure out what I'm going to say and how I can frame it for the next win. I think it's been good for our teams to see a little of my emotion. They see me excited about what we do together. The longer I coach, the better I think through emotion. They need to see that I'm wired. I hope they're thinking, *He was excited about how we played together.*

In the spring of 2017, *Men's Journal* published a feature that described me as the "loosest coach in America." I've taken some ribbing about that, but I actually take a lot of pride in that line. There's no reason for a coach to be a pain in the butt for two or three hours every day with his players. So if we can have some success and have some fun, we'll learn a little bit about ourselves and how to be good teammates. And basketball is going to provide every possible emotion and give all of us every chance to deal with success and adversity on a daily basis.

Keeping It Loose

1

From the Mock Turtle to the Open Collar

I WORE A TIE THE WHOLE TIME I WAS ON THE DUKE STAFF AND MY first two years as head coach at Delaware. Then, of course, when I got out to Notre Dame, everybody thought the mock turtleneck was some sort of fashion statement. If you really do your homework on me, I'm not really a fashion statement guy. It was all for comfort reasons. When I was coaching at Delaware, it was in the America East Conference and it was a bus league. A lot of times those bus rides were six hours to Boston University and Northeastern, and it was just a more comfortable way to travel.

In my third year at Delaware when we won our first league championship, we started playing really well. And, man, I'm superstitious, so I decided to keep wearing the mock turtleneck. Then we won it again my fourth year and in my fifth year we got to the championship game. So I figured, *I'm riding this out, man. This is the look, and it's comfortable.* Even for a home game, you could go out to dinner afterward and you were comfortable.

It's really like the quarter zip that guys wear to press conferences now. And, gosh, it was comfortable. So I stayed with it. When I came to Notre Dame, I heard an awful lot about it. People said: "You are not going to be able to do that at Notre Dame, you cannot do that at Notre Dame."

I did have a tie on at my introductory press conference. I'm not a real style guy and I didn't know much about suits. So David

Haugh, the *Chicago Tribune* columnist, said I dressed like a high school history teacher. It was a great comment. It was kind of a dig, but it's also a little bit of what you see is what you get.

But when the games started, I went back to the mock turtleneck. There was a little pushback from the old guard on that. What was really cool is athletic director Kevin White defended me to some people. I don't think it was this crazy powerful push, and he never said anything to me. But I would get letters—some scathing stuff, saying things like, "That is not a good look. That's not the Notre Dame way. A Notre Dame coach wears a tie." I got a bunch of that. People even sent me ties in the mail.

Then in his first year at our basketball banquet, Jack Swarbrick, White's successor, pulled off his shirt and coat and he had a mock on. It was almost like he was saying it was okay, and he was endorsing me.

I have to admit, I look back at some of the colors I chose back then—like a maroon one and an orange one. *My taste, oh my God.* I look at some pictures that circulate every now and then and I go, *What were you thinking?* We played Maryland in the BB&T Classic one year, and I was into wearing a black suit with a black mock. I'm in all black. The Maryland fans on the baseline are going, "What is this? *A Night at the Roxbury*?" That was the funny movie based off the *Saturday Night Live* skit where two nerdy guys played by Will Ferrell and Chris Kattan try to dress up in suits and T-shirts to pick up women.

One of the great mock stories was at Boston College, and we were in a dog fight. Al Skinner was the Boston College coach, Matt Carroll was on our team, and the game went to overtime. The BC student section was right at the edge of our bench just like it is now at Conte Forum. It's the only time I have ever reacted to a student section. They were on my butt, yelling: "Wear a tie,

Brey. You've got to wear a tie, you no-class such and such." They were all over me.

We had it won with about seven seconds left. We were up six and we were shooting a free throw. So I kind of slowly walked down to the end of the bench, and they were still on me a little bit. And I turned and I said, "How do you like my tie now?" And there were some BC football guys trying to jump the rail. They were coming at me until security got them. I quickly scurried back and sat down. And assistant Sean Kearney gave me this look and said, "What did you say down there?" And I told him, "I shouldn't have said that. I was really stupid, but I had to retaliate one time."

It was definitely not a fashion statement. It was about comfort. What was really great about it, though, is I would go in to buy some clothing in the mall or at Men's Wearhouse, and salespeople would say to me, "Coach, we're selling a lot of mocks. A lot of guys really like your look." And they were serious. I would think, *Holy crap. It's not that cool.*

Wives came up to me and said, "Coach, I want you to know my husband is really going with your look. It's comfortable; he really likes it." I'm thinking, *You have got to be kidding me. Am I starting some kind of movement in town?* But it was a thing.

Finally, about four or five years ago, my daughter, Callie, came up to me before the first game of the season. "Dad, the mock is done," she said. "Dad, can I just talk to you honestly?" It was an intervention. She said, "Look, man, I love you. I root for your team. I never comment much on stuff. I've got your back, but you've got to change it up, man. You've got to go to an open-collar dress shirt. You don't have to wear a tie. I'm not telling you to wear a tie, but go open collar."

So I started wearing open-collar shirts with a sport coat. And she kept on me and so did my son, Kyle.

Our marketing staff in 2017–18 decided to go for a throwback mock night. Well, I had given all of mine to Salvation Army. They are gone. I have none. So I went out to the mall and I walked in a store, and the guy said, "Coach, what are you doing here?"

I said, "Do you have any mock turtlenecks?"

He said, "Oh, I don't know. If we have any, they'd be back there in the corner on that bottom shelf."

I said, "Thanks." And I was trying to hide. I had my hat on. I walked back, found an XL and a large—one in gray and one in black. I wore the gray one with a black suit on the throwback night. Of course, they are still hanging in my closet.

Now when someone wears the mock to coach, everybody else says, "Oh, you've got the Mike Brey look." We played Niagara here in South Bend when Joe Mihalich, who is a former DeMatha assistant and a good friend, broke out the mock in the game. He came right over and said, "What do you think?"

Jerry Wainwright from DePaul came over once, too. He wore a mock turtleneck. Leonard Hamilton, the Florida State coach, still wears them.

I even got some comments when we did the throwback mock night in 2017. Some people in town said, "Maybe you should go back to that."

And I said, "Stop, just stop."

The Notre Dame Way

WHAT WE REALLY TRY TO SELL AT NOTRE DAME—AND IT'S BEEN very successful—is a free-flowing offensive style of play, where a player can read and react and not be put in the box and be robotic. And we recruit guys with a high basketball IQ. You can't have a wide-open kind of react offense without guys who have some innate basketball feel and who can catch and pass. That's why we recruit big guys who are good with the ball. So that has been a real selling point. We are able to flow. We shoot it. We let it rip. Guys play with a free mind. They play confidently and fearlessly.

What we've really sold—and I think the senior class in 2017–18 was yet another example—is that guys get better here. If you invest with us, you are going to be here four or five years. We're not doing the one-and-dones. It's not always going to be easy, but if you hang with us, you're going to get better. What I have loved is we've had guys who have had great senior years the old-fashioned way.

When prospects are on campus visiting, I have video clips of our guards flowing, free-wheeling, shooting it with confidence from the perimeter. It's our offensive style of play. I have edits of our big guys who touch the ball all over the floor. We don't just put you on the block. You get to touch and catch it. You may even bring it up after a rebound. You may not throw an outlet; you may be able to bring it up.

We have an NBA-like screen-and-roll game. We actually have a quote that I use on the highlight tape for guards, and it's a scout saying, "Brey ball is really NBA ball." We throw that up on the TV before we show the video. We have great archives on our offensive style of play. It's free flowing and it's a system you get better in because you are allowed to do things outside of the box. The sexiness of our offensive style of play has been a big selling point.

There's no question we look for guys who can make a shot and stretch the floor. We want guys who can shoot it and score. We want big guys who can open up the floor. Our biggest thing is spacing. You can't have good spacing unless you have shooting threats on the floor. They won't be respected because the defense will play in the lane. But if you have four threats on the floor at one time, man, your spacing is good. Then, if you do throw it in the post, they can't help. You have driving opportunities because defenses are hugging shooters on the other side.

So I feel like we really have established an identity, and that's great. When I go on the road recruiting now, I will be sitting at a game, and we'll be watching somebody play. And other coaches will come up to me and say, "Well, there must be a great shooter playing in the next game if you're here."

Phil Martelli, the longtime St. Joseph's coach, said to me at a recruiting event, "Hey, I just saw a guy that's definitely a Notre Dame guy. He's just going to Notre Dame. Can you just get it over with?"

I was sitting, watching Robby Carmody in the summer of 2017. Brad Brownell, the Clemson head coach, was there watching him play when he made a bunch of shots and he turned to me and said, "Carmody is out there playing and he looks a lot like Steve Vasturia. So you're telling me I've got to deal with another Vasturia?"

We beat some very strong programs for Class of 2018 power forward Nate Laszewski. He chose us in part because we play stretch fours. I can show footage of guy after guy who was a stretch forward for us and how Bonzie Colson developed into that. Our style of play won out on that.

I'm fortunate that now I've been at Notre Dame for a while and I have finally started to have guys who played for me who are now ready to be assistant coaches. I was anxiously awaiting the time to be able to put the staff together like we have it now.

Ryan Ayers and Ryan Humphrey were warming up in the bullpen for me, and then one day a couple of years ago, I had two guys—Anthony Solomon to Georgetown and Martin Ingelsby to Delaware—leave for other coaching jobs. It was an unbelievable perfect storm of getting your guys back.

I had Sean Kearney and Gene Cross before that. We've always had a really good staff here. But it's really neat now that I am able to pick from a pool of my former players. And so when a Rod Balanis leaves to be a head coach, we've got an Eric Atkins there being trained, and you've got some other guys out there who will reach out and may want to come back.

I tried to hire Chris Quinn, but he is on the NBA track. He's going to be an NBA head coach someday, and we're really proud of him. But it's so powerful right now to watch Harold Swanagan, Humphrey, Ayers, and Atkins interact with our current guys, knowing they all have been through all the same things at Notre Dame.

Sometimes they can do some things that I can't. They can have some one-on-one conversations that accomplish some things I can't get done by myself. In 2017–18 the T.J. Gibbs-Atkins relationship was really cool. These guys have been through it all, and it's really a powerful setting to watch. These guys know.

They get it. They believe in the program. They're loyal. Certainly one of the biggest strengths is they all played for me and can translate. If a guy's struggling with his role or maybe doesn't understand something I'm trying to communicate to them, my assistants can translate because they have been through it all. For this era of players at Notre Dame, I often tell them, "You don't know how lucky you are to have these four former guys around."

And we're lucky to have such great connections to the past. A legend named Franny Collins served as a great D.C.-to-Notre Dame connection for me. He was in the DeMatha gym a lot. I never really knew him when I was playing at DeMatha, even though he was around then. But when I was coaching with Morgan Wootten, he was always there. He was bird-dogging the whole area like he always did.

He went to Georgetown, and he and former Notre Dame coach Johnny Dee were old Army buddies. So he started bird-dogging for Dee, even though Collins didn't go to Notre Dame. And then Digger picked it up and nurtured the relationship. And Collins wanted to help. He was empowered.

Coach Wootten had introduced him to me and told me his background. Collins would come to a practice or a game, and I'd see him afterward, so I had a relationship with him. After practice one day at DeMatha, he came up to me. I was just 24. He was always dressed really well and he opened his coat and pulled out a big pen. He said, "Do you know Austin Carr, Adrian Dantley, Sid Catlett?" He was going through all these Notre Dame players from the D.C. area. "They all signed with Notre Dame with this pen."

I said, "Wow, Mr. Collins, that's unbelievable. All those guys?"

He said, "I was there for every one of them."

I said, "Man, you're good."

So it was so neat that I got the Notre Dame job, and his best advice to me was, "Don't change. Don't ever change. Just please keep being yourself."

We would get him great seats behind the bench when we played at Georgetown during Big East play. Even in the waning years when his eyesight wasn't good, he would come with former Notre Dame forward Collis Jones, and Collis would tell him what was going on.

It meant so much to me. The D.C. pipeline guy—whom I knew when I was the young JV coach and history teacher—was now sitting behind the bench, and I was the head coach at Notre Dame. I always felt so proud, and we won at Georgetown a bunch back in the day. I always felt so good when we could win for our D.C. fans. Certainly, that meant a lot to me, but even more because Collins was there for it, and then he would send me an email about the game.

I felt really close to all those guys. Former Irish forward Tracy Jackson and I were the same year in school. We played against each other when he was at Paint Branch High School. The pressure I felt was that I wanted the D.C. pipeline guys to be proud. Those guys were like, "All right, Mike, get it done for us. Get us going again." So when a guy like Collis emails you and he says that he's proud of the group, that makes me excited about what we're doing.

It was really neat my first summer after getting the Notre Dame job. I went back to the High Point Summer League—back when you could still watch high school stuff—in Adelphi, Maryland. I called up Collis and Bob Whitmore, and they got Adrian Dantley, so I walked into the gym with those three guys. Never have I been more proud. The gym was buzzing. I came in with three of our big-time D.C. guys, and we watched the game. It was really, really powerful.

I certainly knew those guys and I've gotten to know them even better now. We all went to Dantley's Basketball Hall of Fame induction, and I think it meant a lot to him. Dantley's always had a special spot because we're both DeMatha guys. So he's always been supportive.

I can't say enough about John Paxson, the Chicago Bulls' executive vice president; he has been really supportive and communicates a lot. It means a lot coming from him based on who he is and what he's done in basketball. He'll text me and check in after a tough loss. It just feels good that he's proud of our program. So many of those guys have been great. Kelly Tripucka had our NCAA games on radio in Brooklyn a couple years ago.

I get really proud when that old guard of guys who were really good here say, "Man, it's awesome to watch our program again." That's the ultimate endorsement. When those guys reach out and are proud, that makes me feel really good; that's what it's all about. The '90s were tough. Not a lot of those guys probably were talking much about having played at Notre Dame.

But I think we've really gotten some guys back on the bandwagon. You get to know them informally through the reunions. And some of their kids have come to school here now at Notre Dame. We'd see Bill Hanzlik and Rich Branning because they were back on campus. All those guys have been so supportive, and that's the key. When the former players before me are talking us up, man, that's powerful. That means a lot to me. I always felt some pressure because I want them to be proud of what we're doing here, so they can wear their Notre Dame stuff into work after a big win and say, "Hey, man, ACC champions," or, "Hey, we beat Syracuse last night."

I feel we've gotten that back, I really do. And that's as gratifying as anything out there because I really respect the guys who came through here before me. I idolized and watched all of them play as a young guy and I imitated them out on the playground. So it's been really cool to see those guys.

During my introductory press conference at Notre Dame, Toni Ginnetti of the *Chicago Sun-Times* asked about this job being a stepping-stone. I said, "I hope I'm good enough to retire here."

I always looked at it as a place you could be really good and stay—and not take another job. Maybe it didn't exactly look like it when I showed up, right? But as I got into it more, I always felt there was a comfort level with the mission. I knew the kind of kids we were going to recruit. I understood all that.

I quickly understood our culture on campus and what kind of young men could fit into that culture. The kind of kids you get here is why you stay. I had Bonzie and Matt Farrell at breakfast one day during their senior seasons, just catching up. I'm talking to them like men. They're just so refreshing to be around.

As I grew to know the culture, I grew to know some of the hurdles, but I never dwelled on what we didn't have. Here's what we've got. I think we've got great selling points, a Big East, ACC style of play. Let's just grind. Let's just work. The two athletic directors who I've been with have been really supportive in that aspect, always asking, "How can we help? What else do you need?"

As I got into years six, seven, and eight, it became a little challenging because those were NIT years. But then we started going back to the NCAA Tournament on a regular basis and we have a system in place. Then the ACC kind of took it to another level of comfort. Why would I want to coach anywhere else? I turned 59 last spring and I'd love to keep coaching until I'm 65.

And the contract I signed in April 2018 gives me the chance to do that. Athletic director Jack Swarbrick and I started talking about this extension last summer. The contract runs through 2025, when I'll be 66. Maybe then it's time for something else. The goal was always to retire here. I casually said that the day of my opening press conference on July 14, 2000. You want to do a good enough job that this is the last stop. Even when we only made it to the NIT, I always said, "It's a great situation. Don't mess with it. Don't overanalyze it and keep plugging." I'm a Midwest guy now because, man, I've been out here so long.

The Chase to 400

2017–18 (21–15, 8–10 ACC)

NIT: W 84–63 vs. Hampton, L 73–63 vs. Penn State

ACC Tournament: W 67–64 vs. Pittsburgh (first round), W
    71–65 vs. Virginia Tech (second round), L 88–70 vs. Duke
    (quarterfinal)

Starters:

   G   T.J. Gibbs, So., 6'3", 15.3 points

   G   Rex Pflueger (captain), Jr., 6'6", 8.0 points

   G   Matt Farrell (captain), Sr., 6'1", 16.3 points

   F   Bonzie Colson (captain), Sr., 6'6", 19.7 points

   C   Martinas Geben (captain), Sr., 6'10", 11.1 points

THE 2017–18 SEASON WAS A CRAZY YEAR FEATURING A TON OF injuries to what was a talented, senior-laden roster I had great expectations for. Bonzie Colson missed 15 games because of a fracture in his left foot that ended up needing surgery, Matt Farrell missed five games with a sprained left ankle during a seven-game stretch in January, and D.J. Harvey missed the final 17 games with a knee injury that required surgery.

I also began the season with 382 victories—11 wins behind legendary Irish head coach Digger Phelps on the list for career victories at Notre Dame. I got Nos. 386, 387, and 388 during the

Maui Invitational. The theme I generated in Hawaii was based on where our program was and the respect it deserves. We needed to be on the wall of champions in the Lahaina Civic Center in Maui. We were so ready to compete over there with an older group. The energy coming out of the locker room was amazing, and in the final, we pulled off an amazing second-half comeback—after trailing 37–23 at halftime—to defeat Wichita State 67–66 on November 22.

I drew up an out-of-bounds play with three seconds left in the game, and Martinas Geben was fouled and sent to the free-throw line. He sank both shots to get us the win, even though we led for just 22 seconds. The veteran trio of Geben, Colson, and Farrell came up huge. Colson led the team with his fourth double-double of the season, scoring 25 points and grabbing 11 rebounds. Farrell scored 15 points, stole an inbounds pass, and dished an assist to Colson to cut the Shockers' lead with less than a minute remaining in regulation, and was named the Maui Invitational MVP following the game.

To come back after being dead in the water against Wichita State and win it like that was awesome. It was a great celebration after the game. I took my shirt off and went in the locker room with a lei on. A picture of that went viral, but it was just a spur-of-the-moment thing. I'd already been in shorts and a T-shirt during the games. In coaching you tend to keep yourself a little bit distant. But I went down on the beach and smoked a cigar with my assistants. Our hotel was rocking, and it was a nice time for our players and their families who came over. You just felt good about that. It will end up being one of the great memories of their sporting lives.

No. 390 was a blast from the past. On December 9 I returned to the Bob Carpenter Center in Newark, Delaware, where I spent my first five seasons as a head coach. Also, my former players were now on the Delaware staff, too. Blue Hens head coach Martin Ingelsby was my point guard my first year and then coached with me for 13. His assistant, Torrian Jones, also played under me. Even Steve Vasturia was in the crowd (as were Rex Pflueger's parents). Heck, I could've conducted an alumni scrimmage. Before the game I told the team: "We've got to get back to rebounding the ball. Let's get our blockouts handled and then get out and go. Back on the backboards, back on the backboards."

Ingelsby's club led 19–17 before T. J. Gibbs turned it around with a traditional three-point play after a layup followed by a three-point field goal—with all that prompting Ingelsby to call time.

We hit four straight shots to end the half with an 11-point lead. "Way to finish," I said during halftime. "Really good stuff out of the double team. Let's keep controlling the board and get out there. But if we don't have it in transition, don't force it, make them guard us a little. We're gonna get you some touches at the elbow. We've done a good job defensively making them take tough shots."

There were six ties and seven lead changes in the opening half, but we closed on a 27–13 run. Gibbs scored 14 of his 21 points in the first half, and Farrell had 14 of his 24 in the second. Colson finished with 19 points and a dozen rebounds, and Geben added a dozen more. Pflueger added 10 points—all in the second half. We shot it well. We played fast, pushed it on purpose, and won 92–68. It's safe to say this was maybe as emotional as a postgame handshake line gets. I couldn't go anywhere without a camera in the vicinity and a greeting from an old friend. And up in the rafters, I saw those two America East title banners and NCAA Tournament appearances.

I tied Digger during our opening game in ACC play and racked up No. 393 with a win against Georgia Tech. We outscored the Yellow Jackets 45–31 over the last 20 minutes. Colson put together a monster performance, scoring 22 points and grabbing 17 boards. And four other guys—Geben (12), Pflueger (11), Farrell (10), and Gibbs (10) all scored in double figures to help get us the 68–59 victory in our last game of 2017, just one day before New Year's Eve.

On January 3, we were back at it with a chance for me to break the record. More significantly, it was the first game for us since Colson went out with a foot injury. It was a frigid night, and the snow howled outside Purcell Pavilion as we faced North Carolina State. Colson stood on the sidelines in street clothes during warmups, chatting up our ops guy, Harold Swanagan. I had our normal three keys to offense and defense: talk in transition, guard your guy, and limit them to one and done on defense. I also wanted to stretch the Wolfpack in transition, control the tempo, and crash the glass on offense. I emphasized that we didn't need to be different because Colson was out. I told them, "We do not need to get outside our roles. Do what we do. Keep moving that ball."

Already missing Colson, Farrell went down in a heap under the basket with an ankle injury with around five minutes left in the first half. We were playing combinations and lineups we didn't think we'd try until next year. With Farrell out, Gibbs became the primary ballhandler and had 22 points and five assists. Taking Colson's spot was Harvey, who had 17 on the night.

Despite losing Farrell in the first half, we led 48–36 at halftime after shooting 61 percent from the floor. Our fans gave us a standing ovation. I told our team, "Hell of a half, man, hell of a half. Way to attack. Way to outcompete their butts. We've got 19 deflections. We're doing a good job on the ball screens, we're doing a good job switching when we need to. Let's keep attacking."

We ended up winning 88–58 to get us to 12–3. Digger presented me with a ceremonial basketball, a commemorative video played on the board, and a banner dropped from the rafters. I received a smaller framed version from athletic director Jack Swarbrick. As soon as the game ended, the 393 banner on the catwalk flipped to 394. Everybody in the locker room wore a COACH BREY 394 shirt. "This will always be a great memory, not because of 394 and the record," I told my team after the game. "It was what we went through in the last couple of days, losing Bonzie, and then Matty goes down halfway through the game. You just played fabulously and fearlessly, and everybody contributed. It's like we reinvented ourselves in 24 hours, and I thought it would take a while. Let's just keep plugging, fellas. Let's be a great story. We got the makeup to do that. I love that this team was the team that got me over the hump."

Win No. 400 came at home against Pittsburgh on February 28, but there were more important things. It marked the return of Colson and the end of the line at home for the seniors. Colson had missed the previous 15 games due to a foot injury and was out there two hours before tip, shooting 10-foot jumpers with assistant coaches Ryan Humphrey and Ryan Ayers. Colson's younger sister, Sydni, sang "The Star Spangled Banner." The Lithuanian national hymn ("Tautiska giesme") played prior to the national anthem, and students waved tiny Lithuanian flags. A larger version hung from the catwalk above the Pitt bench. That all came as a tribute to Geben, a native of Lithuania.

I was excited to have Colson back, and on the white board, I wrote: "Keep letting it rip!"

It was exciting to have the lineup we started early in the season. I wanted us to read, react, and take good shots. I told Colson, "Just nice and easy, man, just play. We don't need to force anything."

Colson finished with a dozen points, nine rebounds, and three blocks in 21 minutes on the floor. Trainer Skip Meyer had talked before the game about 20 minutes being the expectation, and Bonzie basically hit that number. In their final home games, Geben nearly had a double-double, Farrell finished with 14 points, and Matt Gregory got to hoist several shots. Gibbs also had a noteworthy evening, finishing with 14 points.

After we won 73–56, a video with all the seniors played on the board, and the team stood arm in arm for one last playing of the alma mater. It was a special night. I was especially proud of the fact that the seniors had now totaled 100 career wins. I told them, "We couldn't have scripted it any better—how we got started, how we played, and how well our seniors played. What a great memory for you guys—and you deserve it."

We had to face Pittsburgh again in the first round of the ACC Tournament, and that 67–64 win set us up to face an NCAA Tournament-bound Virginia Tech team. We trailed 34–21 at halftime. "We played like crap in that half and we're only down 13," I told my guys at the break. "We'll get moving and get our looks in the second half, so we'll have a shot at this thing. But we're going to have to work defensively and we can't make mistakes. You didn't think it was going to be easy tonight, did you? It's going to be hard as heck the last 20 minutes. Empty the tank!"

And so they did. But it got worse before it got better. We trailed by 21 before finally kicking into gear. Three straight makes from beyond the arc on successive possessions powered a 17–3 spree to cut the deficit to just four points at 54–50 with 7:45 left. Gibbs and Farrell each scored five points in that stretch. A Colson three-pointer at the end of the shot clock gave us a 60–59 lead with two minutes left. We scored 50 points on 12-of-21 shooting in the second half, including seven threes, to win 71–65. "Just like we drew it up, right?" I joked to reporters after the game.

That was win No. 402, but more importantly it gave us a chance at possibly earning an NCAA Tournament berth. Ayers at halftime told strength coach Tony Rolinski he would do chin-ups on a bar in the locker room if Notre Dame came back and won. He made good on that and did 21—one for each point of the comeback—of them. I was proud of my team for coming back. "What a great win, what a great, gutsy win," I told them. "This was a huge game for a lot of reasons. We were getting our butts kicked for a while, but we hung in there, and our defense was fabulous in the second half."

Duke knocked us off the next night, and ultimately the NCAA Selection Committee left us out. I turned the page quickly after we did not get into the NCAA Tournament. I knew we were close, and Jack Swarbrick later told me that Bernard Muir, a member of the NCAA committee, called him the night of the selections to let him know we were the last team out. The NCAA committee has a policy to contact those last four teams out, but Jack knew I didn't need to hear that then. I was not disappointed; it was almost as if that was our fate that year. The chairman of the committee was Creighton athletic director Bruce Rasmussen. I ran into him at the National Association of

Basketball Coaches meeting after the season, and he thanked me for how we handled that.

After the end of our season, I went to the Final Four. I always like attending it because you gain insight from the other coaches on what kind of year you had. But the coaches were thoroughly confused about how to talk to me in San Antonio. Some said, "You made a run" or "I've never seen anything like that in terms of the injuries you had." Others said, "You really came off the mat" or "Tough luck." It was all over the board.

I think about how we started at Maui, winning that championship in maybe the most prestigious of the preseason tournaments and reaching fifth in the polls. Then I think about losing seven in a row and getting on that plane in Raleigh, North Carolina, after getting beat pretty good by North Carolina State. It was February 3, and we were 13–10 and 3–7 in the league at that point. Then I think about coming off the mat to beat Virginia Tech in Brooklyn in the ACC Tournament in the biggest comeback in the history of our program. Then we actually got into the NCAA bracket for a day and a half until Davidson won its Atlantic 10 Tournament in an upset, knocking us out an hour before the announcement. So we had a little bit of everything happen.

This team didn't win an ACC championship, didn't go to the Elite Eight, and didn't even go to the NCAA Tournament. But it will always have a special spot in my heart, starting with the leadership of the senior class in terms of being rock solid and setting a tone. In the midst of that seven-game losing streak, I said to them, "Any of you here signed up for the class at Notre Dame titled Handling Adversity 101? There actually isn't one, but you're in one now." Another day I told them, "Because of who we had coming back, especially Colson and Farrell, we're on national television a lot down the stretch. Everyone is going to watch how we handle this. They are going to see who we are and how we deal with this."

I give our guys a heck of a lot of credit for handling things like men. This will be a reference point in their lives—they're going to come up against it at some point and they'll come back to how they had each other's back, how they picked each other up, and how they found positives in tough times.

Growing Up
on the Beltway

MY FATHER, PAUL, WAS A CAREER ATHLETIC DIRECTOR, COACH, and physical education teacher at the junior high and high school levels. My mother, Betty, swam at Purdue; competed at the 1956 Olympic Games in Melbourne, Australia, in the butterfly; and then became a swim coach. And for years my parents ran the pool in the summers at the Columbia Country Club in Maryland. So the Breys' dinner table talk was athletics and teaching. I grew up in gyms and around pools. I was a true product of my environment.

I went to a lot of University of Maryland basketball games when I was young. I went to Baltimore Bullets games because my dad had a season-ticket package. My dad coached junior high basketball, and I was kind of their team manager. When I was eight, nine, or 10 years old or so, sitting on the bench with my dad's eighth-grade team was a thrill. In elementary school my mom would get me out of school early to be the orange slice guy. I would get to sit on the end of the bench. Those junior high players were like NBA guys to me. I lived and died with that team.

I grew up a Duke fan because my uncle, Jack Mullen, played basketball at Duke in the early 1960s. There are pictures of me on Art Heyman's shoulders in the Cole Field House locker room after a Duke-Maryland game.

I had my uncle's jersey, No. 20. He was such an inspiration for me as a young kid. He lifeguarded for my dad at the pool, so he was almost like a big brother.

His son, Steve, is three years younger than I am, and we'd shoot around at my house. When they were over visiting, my uncle let us shoot for about 20 minutes and then he'd open up the door and say, "All right, the varsity is coming out now." He'd come down the steps, and we'd play him two on one. We were just thrilled to be out there with him.

I played in the rec leagues and was just around basketball all the time. I didn't think about anything else. I wanted to coach at the high school level because Morgan Wootten was such a role model for me at DeMatha Catholic High School and because my dad was a high school educator. I thought I'd end up trying to go to one of the Montgomery County, Maryland, public schools because that was a high-paying public school system, the best in the area. Could I ever get the Churchill High School job in Potomac and run a camp in the summer? It wouldn't be a bad gig.

The Bullets played 10 games at Cole Field House, and we saw Wilt Chamberlain and the Los Angeles Lakers. Back in those days, I could stand outside the Lakers' locker room or the Bullets' locker room in that tunnel at Cole. We would high-five Wilt and all those guys. When I later became an assistant at Duke, I'd have flashbacks to when I was standing there in that same tunnel.

The other thing my dad did was take his junior high team to the high school state championships every year at Maryland. On a Friday starting at 10:00 AM, they ran the games one after another at Cole. The field trip for his team would be to go for the whole day, and I always went along. We would watch all five games.

It seemed like I lived at Cole Field House. I went to Lefty Driesell's camp. I'd always go to the city championship game. I was there when DeMatha would play against the D.C. public school champ. We got tickets to the North Carolina-Maryland game at Cole. I was just around basketball all the time, and the dinner table talk was about what happened with all these different basketball teams. Once I was a high school player, Uncle Jack would come over and watch me and critique me. He also would beat me one on one in basketball. I was saturated with the sport every day.

Both my parents really had a competitive edge. There's no question about that. My mom really was unbelievable in that regard, which was very good for me to be around. You don't get to be an Olympian like she was without that, and there really were no organized women's sports back then. That was passed along to me, though I don't know if it was healthy all the time because I was looking to beat somebody in something every day. But it certainly was conducive to the line of work I chose. It was really a heck of an environment to grow up in. And all the kids came to our house and they really gravitated to my parents.

I always said the great thing about being the son of an athletic director and PE teacher was that you had all the equipment. We had a pitching rubber and a home plate in our backyard. We played Wiffle Ball back there. We had a basketball hoop and all the football gear—the helmets and pads. It was a great, unbelievable childhood. I played Little League football up until eighth grade. I was the quarterback and I also played baseball until seventh grade. And then I got the hoops bug, and basketball became a year-round activity due to the camps in the summer.

My parents were both employees of Montgomery County in Maryland. My dad was a career educator, and after we grew up, my mom went back to teaching in Montgomery County. I attended public schools there through elementary and junior high, but at age nine, I started going to Morgan Wootten's camp at the old Metropolitan Area Basketball School at St. John's High School. Wootten, the DeMatha coach, and Joe Gallagher, the St. John's coach, were the two legendary coaches from the big rival programs. In the summer, though, they ran this basketball camp together. It was probably one of the first basketball camps in the United States. It was a day camp at St. John's, and the DeMatha and St. John's basketball players were the counselors.

Just being there in that environment with the DeMatha and St. John's guys was awesome. The high school guys played a staff game at lunch, and the campers like me sat in the stands and watched. Those guys really went at it, and we marveled at them. And DeMatha's finest, Adrian Dantley, was a regular guest speaker at the camp. He was my first coach at Metropolitan when I was nine and was already a star at DeMatha then. My mom always kept the report card he filled out on me.

My dad used to worry about me all the time because I would be running all day. A lot of times I didn't eat because it was so hot. The heat index would reach 104. My dad would say, "We've got to get you something different to eat at lunch. You're wasting away."

When I was in high school, we played in the staff game. I was on my feet coaching all the time. In any free time I did get, I would play one on one against one of the St. John's guys and then play the summer league game at night. It was great to be able to play all the time. So at this very young age, I was around all these DeMatha and St. John's players, and Coach Wootten lectured every day. I was kind of under his tutelage and I went every summer. Later my mom let me go to two sessions, and I would have gone the whole summer.

The pool at Columbia Country Club was right around the corner, not far from St. John's. For their summer job, my parents taught swimming and ran the swim club. They dropped me off and picked me up. I would come by the pool and grab a hamburger and then go home with my dad.

I was so impressionable back then and I had been around the DeMatha guys and around Coach Wootten so much. So when I was 12 or 13, I started asking my dad if could I go to DeMatha. I was in the public school system and I would have gone to Woodward High School with a lot of good friends. We had a really good group of guys who were good basketball players. We won our junior high championship. My family actually lived in Rockville, Maryland, in Montgomery County, and DeMatha was in Prince George's County, which is probably 25 miles away.

Even after all this exposure to DeMatha and my love for the school, there was some question where I would go to high school. It wasn't automatic that DeMatha would be the decision, but my parents were so great about it. My mom understood it because she knew she had to get to the best places to train when she was an Olympic swimmer. She said, "That's what he needs to do. We've got to do it." The tuition in 1975 at DeMatha was $700. That was a lot of money back then. I remember hearing my parents talking about that and that they could make it up doing swimming lessons.

Pete Strickland was two years older than me at DeMatha, and I really looked up to him. Billy Mecca, who later became the longtime athletic director at Quinnipiac, was a tough Matt Farrell-type point guard at DeMatha at the time. Those two guys made big impressions on me. Coach Wootten used to watch guys play and recruit out of the summer camp. I still remember my dad and me talking to him, and he saw my growth at the camp. He said, "Mike can play for us; we'd like to have Mike. If he makes that decision, he's got a chance to play for us." Well, that was the ultimate endorsement, and I'll never forget that.

Going to DeMatha was an unbelievable sacrifice for my parents, but I was really proud. In the 10th grade, my parents dropped me off at a Giant Food Store in Bethesda, which wasn't far from our house—maybe 10 minutes away. Bernie McGregor, who was an assistant coach at DeMatha and taught religion, picked me up. I drove with him from Bethesda to DeMatha in the morning; that was my commute.

Coming home was always an adventure. A lot of times I took a metro bus. I learned how to change buses. I could get as far as Silver Spring, and then my parents picked me up there. Varsity practice went from 3:00 to 5:00 PM, and junior varsity practice was 5:00 to 7:00 PM. I'd get home at 9:00 or 9:30 and turn around and do it again the next day. I played on the DeMatha JV team in 10th grade. And then my junior year, I got a car so I was driving the beltway every day. We had a couple of other DeMatha guys coming from Rockville, and I picked them up, and they helped pay for gas. It was a sacrifice socially because all my buddies I grew up with, who lived in Rockville, were going to Woodward High. I would try and hang out, but they were in a different phase by then.

DeMatha helped me become a better player because of all the extra gym time. It was a little bit of a lonely existence, but I did it and it certainly benefited me. I worked on my game because that's what you were supposed to do. Dantley said to do the same thing.

I had a very good junior year. I was the backup point guard to Tony Ellis, who made a man out of me and played collegiately at Colorado. He kicked my butt every day in practice. He was a tough, 6'1" guard from D.C.

I was the starting point guard my senior year. Things were going along very well, and then I got mononucleosis. It just wiped me out. By the time I came back, I was not going to play because we had Dutch Morley, a junior who eventually played at Maryland, and Sidney Lowe, a 10th grader who would go on to star at North Carolina State. So there was no way I was going to get back in there. It was really a discouraging senior year for me because of my health. Back when I was 11, I honestly thought that I could someday be the starting point guard at DeMatha. I thought I could be the guy.

So all that was really crushing. The only two college offers I still had were from the University of Vermont and Northwestern State University in Natchitoches, Louisiana, and those came about because they had seen me play in the summer at the Five-Star Basketball Camp. I visited Vermont before my senior season. It was Halloween. I'll never forget it. It was a really cool experience, a great visit. Of course, back then I was thinking I was going to start and play my whole senior year of high school. And there was no early signing period at that time. But Vermont's interest just kind of faded after I had mono as a senior.

Because I got sick, I only played in a couple of games for DeMatha. But there was a graduate assistant coach at Northwestern State named Ralph Penn. He stayed in touch with me because he saw me at Five-Star, and I had a really good week at Five-Star before my senior year. I made the All-Star team, and he stayed with me. I thought, *Gosh, somebody still loves me.* I went down to visit in March. It was beautiful, and the weather was nice. They wanted me, and I had a good chance to start. So I decided to enroll there. I never even considered that I would be going all the way to Louisiana, and my parents really weren't ever going to see me play.

I was a backup as a freshman, but I played a lot at Northwestern State. I started my sophomore and junior years and really had a great experience. In the summers when I came back from Louisiana, I worked Coach Wootten's camp every day of the week. I was a director, running it during the day and then at night I coached the DeMatha summer league team. That involved 30 games over the summer. Coach Wootten was great. He would disappear sometimes—almost as if he was saying, *Let's see if Mike can figure this stuff out.*

I ran it along with Jack Bruen—God rest his soul—who played at Power Memorial Academy with Kareem Abdul-Jabbar. Bruen had played at Catholic University and was then the coach at Carroll High School, the other Catholic power at the time and also former Notre Dame president Monk Malloy's alma mater. Bruen later became head coach at both Catholic University and Colgate.

He was like a big brother to me. He was older than I was, but he and I were the co-directors of the camp. He was a great guy to bounce things off of and he had been really key for me getting through my senior year of high school because I was really depressed after my sickness ruined my basketball season. I'd worked so hard and wore myself out. Bruen said, "Don't worry about it. You'll get a good scholarship. I'll help you with that." He was my history teacher as a high school junior. I was with him every day at camp. He was a fun guy and a real personality with charisma.

I had been around Coach Wootten for so long—and now I was doing the lectures that I heard him give so many times. I was running the camp with the DeMatha and St. John's guys and I ran the staff games at lunch. Then I'd grab a quick hamburger from Roy Rogers and go to the summer league and coach great players like Adrian Branch and Danny Ferry on the DeMatha team. Coach Wootten and I talked about the game afterward. Those summers were such a great experience.

At Northwestern State I played for Tynes Hildebrand, a longtime coach and just a typical southern guy. He was very steady and a really good man. We didn't have a very good junior year, and he got fired. Now I was going into my senior year with a new head coach. I didn't know how interested he was going to be in a senior point guard who didn't really win for the head coach who just got fired. The new coach brought in a couple of junior college players, so I decided I was going to transfer.

I could come back and go to George Washington tuition free because my mother was the swim coach there. The other reason I had no problem leaving Northwestern State was that I had talked to Coach Wootten, and he said I should come back home and finish school. He said, "That would be great, and then you can come over and coach the DeMatha freshman team after you're done with class. That's all I want you to do. If you can help me with the varsity, great, but coach your team." My reaction was, "That's awesome."

I came home for the summer and I was still playing pickup ball in addition to running the DeMatha camp and coaching the summer league. I made the decision to go to George Washington, but it was going to take me two years to finish my degree at GW. I was commuting and living back home again, so I was feeling a little bit like a loser.

In September I was playing pickup ball with some GW players. I had gotten to know a couple of them because they were local guys. Bob Tallent, the GW coach, grabbed me. He was standing in a doorway at the Smith Center watching us play and he remembered me from D.C. He said, "Are you in grad school here?" I said, "No, Coach, I'm still trying to finish up and I think I'm going to coach the freshman team at DeMatha."

He said, "Do you have any eligibility?"

I said, "Yeah, I only played three years in Louisiana."

And he said, "You know what, we could use you. You could play here."

I think he appreciated the idea of a one-year guy—sitting a year, playing a year—because he did the same thing when he left after his junior year at Kentucky with Adolph Rupp. He was a great talent out of the state of Kentucky, transferred to GW, sat a year, played a year, and had a great senior year. Plus, he knew I was a local guy. I think he thought that might help him recruit in the area, including at DeMatha.

I called Coach Wootten and I said, "Coach Tallent thinks I could play for him. I know I only have one year left and I'm not going to be a pro, but I just have to get it out of my system." Coach was great. He said, "Absolutely, you need to do it. We'll get you back in camp in the summer. You'll coach the summer league again. This will be here when you're done. I totally understand."

So I sat out that whole year, and it was great. Playing for a lot of different head coaches wasn't fun at the time, but it was very educational because I learned three different philosophies: Coach Hildebrand's at Northwestern State, the Adolph Rupp system Tallent had learned, and Tallent's own system. Then I was ready to play, but spring came along, and the school fired Tallent. So back-to-back years, two coaches who were great to me—Hildebrand and Tallent—were fired. So I decided to finish my fourth year and then go back for my fifth year to finish up and coach the freshman team at DeMatha.

Meanwhile, my old DeMatha friend, Pete Strickland, was now playing basketball in Ireland. He called one day and said,

"Get 10 guys, and I can get you an all-expenses-paid trip. You put a team together and you guys are going to play." So I put together a team, we went over there, and it ended up making me ineligible.

Gerry Gimelstob—God rest his soul—ended up getting the head job at GW. He had been an Indiana assistant coach and had won the national championship...with Bob Knight. He tracked me down, even though I wasn't on scholarship; I had a freebie because of my mom's tuition-free deal. Coach called me in and said he had two questions. He said, "First of all, we need you. You're a senior. I need some leadership, and you know the team."

I said, "Coach, I really just want to finish school. I didn't know if you wanted your own guys, some young guys. I'm this old fifth-year point guard. And I want to coach so I'm going to be coaching the DeMatha freshman team."

He said, "No, I need you. I want you playing."

Then he said, "The other question is this: did you play in a tournament in Ireland?"

I said, "Yeah." And he said, "Well, we need to clear that up."

Even though I wasn't on scholarship, I had to sit out three games because I played in three games in Ireland. That was the penalty.

I'll never forget the fourth game. We were playing at Stetson. At the pregame meal, Coach Gimelstob came over to me and said, "Look, I can't start you tonight."

Now he was still a very young coach—this was his first head coaching job. I said, "Oh, you better not start me tonight or there will be a revolt." I was just trying to help him. I said to him again, "If I get a chance to play, I'll be ready."

Dave Hobel, who's a high school coach in Maryland and still a great friend who works our Notre Dame camp, was the deserved starter. But he got two fouls in three minutes that night. I went in and started the rest of the season. I probably played close to 40 minutes a game the rest of the year.

It ended up being really neat. I was back in my hometown and I got to play a ton. We were 13–14 that first year under Gerry Gimelstob. We were respectable. I was the old guy keeping the group together, and Coach was very good to me.

I lived at home because I couldn't really afford to move out. I never thought about doing anything different other than coaching. It was in my genes. My dad was a physical education major and teacher, and my mom was a PE major. Down at Northwestern State, the major was called physical education for coaching. They had coaching methods classes. When I was there for three years, I was into the coaching stuff all the time.

George Washington had a fancy name for it: human kinetics and leisure studies. That was PE, basically, but I was trained as an educator. In the second year of the program, you were out in the schools. Anyway, I finally had my degree, I was done playing basketball, and it was time to get a little more serious about coaching.

Working for DeMatha's
Master Mentor

ONCE I GRADUATED FROM GEORGE WASHINGTON IN 1982, GERRY Gimelstob wanted me to stay as a graduate assistant basketball coach. But I also had been in and around the DeMatha program for a long time, and it looked like I had some sort of future there with Morgan Wootten.

Coach Wootten and I went to Ledo's, our pizza spot. He said, "Mike, here's the thing for your coaching career. Number one, you need your own team. You're going to have the DeMatha junior varsity. You must have your own team if you're going to get into this coaching thing. You're 23 years old. You're going to have your own team and you need that. And then you're going to help me."

Now remember that Coach is a great salesman. He said, "Here's the thing. If you really want to get into college coaching—with all the great players we have—do you know the number of college coaches who will be coming in to recruit DeMatha? You're going to be handling all of them. So if that's what you want to do, your network is going to be unbelievable with us."

He was smart—and he was exactly right. So I went back to DeMatha, coached the JV team for two years, and taught U.S. history. I could teach in a Catholic school, but I was not certified to teach history in a public school. Since I'd taken some social studies classes, they were going to fudge it. I went in to meet John Moylan, the DeMatha principal. I was thinking he was going to grill me about whether or not I could really do this, especially handle the history stuff. But his son had been on the freshman team, and now he was coming to me on the junior varsity. DeMatha had won the league as freshmen, and his son was the starting two guard. John said, "Look, the head of the department will get you all straight with the books and everything else you need, and you'll be fine. Now let me tell you about the team you're inheriting."

We sat for 30 minutes and talked about this player, that player, and the other player. We ended up winning the junior varsity championship that year, and I was all of 23 years old.

It was an unbelievable way to start. Plus, I helped with the varsity, and we had Danny Ferry, who later signed with Duke, and Quentin Jackson and Bennie Bolton, who both went to North Carolina State. So we had some really gifted guys.

When I went back to DeMatha, I was nervous about teaching history. I didn't major in history and I was going to have to get up in front of all these kids and I was only four or five years older than they were. The best advice I got was to just stay one chapter ahead of them. The second year was a lot easier because I had all the lesson plans from the first year. But that first year, I never have been more exhausted from school because I was coaching and I was teaching. It was crazy, but it was great.

I learned how to work hard. You learned how to *really* work. At DeMatha I taught six classes of history and I had to study hard to prepare. There were even 12 bingos a year, and I helped run them because those were big fund-raisers for us. After two years I moved up to work with Coach Wootten on the varsity, and Pete Strickland came in and took over the JV team. So he and I spent three years together as assistants.

Coaching was what I wanted to do. I was just so inspired by my parents, watching them teach, coach, and interact. Then I think about being around Coach Wootten and coming back those summers when I would run the camp and lecture four or five times a day on defense, blocking out, and everything else. I had the DeMatha players demonstrating for me.

We had 300 kids, and it was 98 degrees. I would wake up during camp summers, and if it was raining, I would almost start crying because I knew it was going to be a total circus between rotating teams and everything else. They had four outside courts and only two inside courts. So if it rained, the entire schedule had to be compressed. We'd even have kids doing dribbling drills in the cafeteria after lunch.

But Coach Wootten was great to me. After coaching the summer league games, I'd have a beer and pizza with him afterward. He'd say, "I like what you did there, but here's something to think about." I'd be in the office after camp with Joe Gallagher and Coach telling stories. They'd say, "Hey, Mike, why don't you run out and grab some burgers?" I was the coffee and donuts guy. I would come back, sit with them, and just listen, and they would tell stories forever. I just absorbed it all—and it was unbelievable training. Plus, I could go home and had my parents as educators, too. I was just in such an environment of great teachers and I was so very lucky for that.

I sat there as a 25-year-old high school assistant coach, and Coach Wootten delegated parts of practice for me to run. Dean Smith, Lefty Driesell, Mike Krzyzewski, Digger Phelps—they'd all be there. Talk about an audition. Then at some point Coach tired of handling all the recruiting and setting up the home visits, so I inherited all that. The Duke staff would call one day for their home visit. Then Dean Smith would call back the next day.

He'd say, "Mike, I know you have Danny [Ferry] in class. Any feedback?"

In some ways going to school at DeMatha in the very beginning was a risky move. I probably would have been a starting point guard on a state championship team at Woodward, the public high school in Rockville. But going to DeMatha set me up for everything the rest of the way.

My Notre Dame connections started with Adrian Dantley being my first coach at summer camp. Then there was Ray Smith, a ninth-grade algebra teacher at DeMatha. Smitty was a huge Notre Dame guy; every day he had his big Notre Dame jacket on. He was an absolute die-hard Notre Dame guy with all kinds of personality. He ran a little college football pool for the teachers, and any time Notre Dame lost, there would be 10 teachers down there giving him a hard time.

The Notre Dame karma was coming out of his classroom all the time. He had all kinds of stuff on the wall and he had the jacket that you couldn't miss. He passed away before I could ever get him out here to Notre Dame, though his kids still came out to South Bend a number of times. I still think about what it would have been like if Smitty could have come to visit me here. He would have been beside himself. *The guy across the hall from him teaching history is now coaching for Notre Dame.*

When I was a junior at DeMatha, the Capital Classic All-Star Game was just starting. And Rich Branning from Marina High School in Huntington Beach, California, earned an invitation. Since Coach ran the Capital Classic, he said, "Mike, you've got a car, you're a junior. Rich Branning is going to play in the Capital Classic and he's coming in a couple days early. So could you be their host, run him around, and get him in the gym?"

So I hung out with Rich and his dad. We shot at the DeMatha gym, and I got to know him. Then I idolized him, watching him play at Notre Dame and following him. So the Notre Dame thing was always around. I met Digger when he came to recruit Ferry. I remember former Notre Dame assistant coach Pete Gillen because he coached me at Five-Star Camp. He was the Notre Dame assistant coach I knew the best.

Digger was in the DeMatha gym all the time. I remember introducing myself and talking to him. Austin Carr, Collis Jones, and Sid Catlett were Beltway-area players who went on to Notre Dame. There was Tracy Jackson from Paint Branch. There was Chris "Hawk" Stevens, who played for Digger and later came back to teach in the business school at Notre Dame. It seemed as if there was Notre Dame all over the D.C. area.

Before my fifth year, I tried to get the Churchill High School job in Montgomery County. My dad was wired in there, but I was a physical education major, and the school was not really hiring for PE. I wanted to get an interview for the job, and Churchill was really interested. But I couldn't get a teaching position. I would have taken it and probably would have been coaching in Montgomery County for 35 years—just like my dad.

I came back to DeMatha for one more year. After that fifth season, one interesting opportunity was with Oliver Purnell, who was at Old Dominion. He was another great guy whom I had gotten to know because he was always recruiting DeMatha. He was offered the Kentucky State job and he called and said, "How about coming to be my assistant? It will be like you're the white shadow at Kentucky State."

Purnell didn't end up taking the job, and I'm not sure I was interested in going with him. But we still tease each other that we should have gone to Kentucky State together.

Also after my fifth season at DeMatha, Chuck Swenson had left the Duke staff when he got the William & Mary head coaching job and he was all over me about coming with him. I had really gotten to know the Duke staff well. They were practically living at DeMatha because of Ferry—exactly the way Coach Wootten had suggested. Swenson said, "Why don't you come with me as the full-time guy?" And I seriously thought about it. I was starting to get fairly educated about the business and whom to hitch your wagon to.

I remember going in to Coach Wootten one day about a week after Swenson offered me the position. I said, "Coach, I've got a question for you. Chuck Swenson would love me to come to William & Mary. I'm intrigued about college coaching, and you may think I'm really crazy, but what do you think about his spot at Duke?"

We all had gotten to know Mike K well. Coach Wootten said, "Let's make a run at that." Obviously, Mike K and Morgan had the utmost respect for each other. And having Coach Wootten as your rabbi was unbelievable. I think I lucked out because Mike K wanted someone who was going to be with him a while and not be a quick hit for a head job. So I told Swenson no, made the run at the Duke opening, and I ended up getting the job in Durham.

The Duke Years

I WAS IN SUCH A GREAT PLACE WITH MORGAN WOOTTEN AT DeMatha. I not only learned so much from him, but I also had my own junior varsity team to coach. I did that for two years and what I was doing—like writing up practice plans and having a voice— was really helpful. Then I assisted him on the varsity, and we had so many darn good players, so I was developing relationships with the college assistants and certainly with the head guys, too.

For Mike Krzyzewski, Danny Ferry was the linchpin that swung it for him. Mike K beat North Carolina on a guy. Ferry was down to Duke and Carolina. He signed late, and so Duke was at every one of his games. They did not miss a game; either Mike K, Chuck Swenson, or Bob Bender came to every game. That was unbelievable.

I really developed a close relationship with Swenson and Bender, the two assistants who were doing the legwork. Mike K was so down to Earth. He was great and he always had time for everybody. You felt good when a head coach from the ACC knew your name. After Ferry ended up going to Duke, I went down and worked their camp one summer. I liked my role at DeMatha, but I had been there five years and I was intrigued about opportunities in college.

I talked to Gerry Gimelstob, my college coach at George Washington, and ran past him the idea of taking a shot at the

Duke job that opened when Swenson left. He said, "I think that's a great decision," he said. "In this profession it's about who you hitch your wagon to."

I went into the process at Duke as a total long shot. The other two finalists were Stu Jackson, who was an assistant at Providence with Rick Pitino, and then Mike Hanks, a Bob Knight guy who had just been fired as the head coach at South Alabama. So you figured Knight was really working Mike K for Hanks. Pitino really put in a good word in for Stu.

Then there was a tricky dynamic in that we had a rising senior at DeMatha in Jerrod Mustaf, who ended up going to Maryland. Duke was going to recruit him; everybody was going to recruit him. But if Duke hires Mike Brey, how does that sound? Mike K was struggling with all of that. But there's no question Coach Wootten and Mike K became very close through Ferry's recruitment. Mike K really respected Coach Wooten, who was really selling me.

The thing that probably got it over the hump was that Coach Bender was moving up as kind of the right-hand man to Mike K. He was really comfortable with me because he was going to have to train me, and he and I had really hit it off. Bender was, I think, a difference maker in terms of saying, "I think Mike Brey would be a fit."

I was also fortunate in that Mike K wanted somebody who was going to be with him for a while. I think he looked at Jackson as someone who would be with him for two years and then want a head job because he'd been an assistant for a while and was due. Hanks was older, had been a head coach, and it hadn't worked out. Bender put a good word in, and there's no question with Ferry becoming the best player at Duke that the timing helped. I had a lot of good karma there. So it was like a perfect storm.

When I got the job, I fought a little bit of the thought that, *Well, they hired him to get Mustaf.* That dynamic was there, and I felt a little pressure. We did the home visit with Jerrod, I knew his father, and I had spent a lot of time with the kid. I had just coached the kid for three years. I even drove him home many nights. And the first question the father asked Mike K is why he didn't hire a black assistant. Talk about a tense home visit. Mike K really handled it well. Even though I was the guy getting the job, it wasn't like I was a complete stranger. But we obviously didn't get him; he went to Maryland.

I was with Bender for two years, and then he got the Illinois State job. I'm always indebted to him because he really trained me. The two full-time guys do everything together. I was 27 when I got there. I had five great years with Coach Wootten, but I didn't have the recruiting experience. But I think Mike K knew my people skills and personality. By way of Ferry, he heard how I could connect with guys.

The other connection came in my second meeting with Mike K. He knew about the DeMatha-Carolina link because of the relationship between Coach Wootten and Dean Smith. I said to Mike K, "You gotta understand, I've always been a Duke fan. My uncle played on the 1960 ACC championship team, their first championship team. His name is Jack Mullen."

Mike K responded, "You're kidding me."

So there was a lot of fate there. Mike K said to me, "Mike, I don't want anybody coming down here who doesn't want to be a head coach. You're gonna have your hands on everything."

I'm thoroughly indebted to Mike K because you didn't just recruit as an assistant coach. You did it all, including scheduling, running camps. And so he really got me prepared.

I went down there beginning with the 1987–88 season, and we went to five straight NCAA Final Fours. My second year we won the NCAA regional against Georgetown at the Meadowlands, and I thought to myself, *Wait a minute, this is my second year college coaching, and I'm gonna be on the bench in the Final Four two years in a row? Do you know how many coaches never experience that once?* Driesell, the longtime former Maryland coach, was a guy my family all knew—and he never coached in the Final Four.

Then we went to three more. And then it was six out of eight. It was just an unbelievable run. We had great players and a cool staff. After Bender left for Illinois State, Tommy Amaker came on, and so as I look back at the timing, I was very lucky. The only reason I got in there and got that spot was Mike K didn't have any of his former players quite ready yet. It was all timing. Amaker wasn't quite ready when I came to Durham; he was two years away. If it was another year or two later, I never would have gotten in there because he was then hiring his own guys.

It's funny because he's got a lot of former assistants out there now, but all of them but me played for him. So I'm in a separate category. I'm a former assistant, but the guys who played for him—just like the guys who played for me—hold a special spot in his heart. These guys here with me now at Notre Dame are the same way. So you've got a little asterisk by your name. And, of course, I've been gone a long time.

Amaker came in, and we got to be the best of friends. We were both D.C. guys and so we already knew each other. I actually coached against Amaker when I coached the DeMatha summer league team and Amaker was playing for W.T. Woodson. He had 38 points, and his team beat us; he used to tease me all the time. We were really close.

It was such a magical time. When we're on the road recruiting in the summer now, Mike K and I will end up sitting together six or eight times watching a court. We'll start rehashing memories, funny stories, and all kinds of crazy stuff. One that comes up a lot of is the 1990 NCAA Championship Game in Denver against UNLV. The Runnin' Rebels were coming down the floor and they were just kicking the crap out of us. They ended up beating us by 30—103–73. They were getting down the floor so fast. It was just a beatdown and it was only 10 minutes in.

Phil Henderson was a senior and was the leading scorer for us on that team. He brought it across half court, picked up his dribble, and they were really guarding and pressuring us. It was getting close to a five count, and Henderson just started dribbling again. One of the officials, Ed Hightower, calls double dribble, and now we're going to the media timeout. We felt like, *What else could happen?* We don't look much better than a grade-school team. Then Henderson went over to Hightower with the ball and said he wasn't sure there was enough air in the ball. And Mike K just looked at me. We won 29 games that year, but that's the kind of day it was.

All my experiences at Duke obviously set me up for the rest of my career and made my profile amazingly high. Amaker and I had job offers every year. We were also each other's therapist: "What do we think about this one? We need to go to lunch. I gotta talk to you."

We would be each other's sounding board on what was a good job and what wasn't. We used to say, "You're on the block" when one of us was involved with a job. That was our code phrase, "You look a little tight—are you on the block?"

It's neat seeing all those Duke guys out there now—you've got Chris Collins at Northwestern, Jeff Capel at Pittsburgh, and

Steve Wojciechowski at Marquette. Those were guys I recruited. Bobby Hurley, Johnny Dawkins, Jeff Capel, I see all these guys on the road, and we get together and tell stories. I'm still in touch with Christian Laettner. He checks in, he likes watching our program at Notre Dame.

Yeah, we were spoiled. It was just unreal. We played Michigan in the national championship game in 1992 in Minneapolis. Sidney Lowe, whom I played with at DeMatha, was an assistant with the Minnesota Timberwolves. We beat Indiana in the semifinals, and Michigan beat Cincinnati. So I called Lowe and said we'd like to put a highlight tape together like we do for scouting. But we didn't have the computers to do it or machines on the road. So Pete Gaudet, our restricted earnings coach, and I went over there and I said, "We need to sit with your editing guy. Can we work with him for an hour or so?" He said, "Come on over." So we went over in the morning on the day between games and cut up the Michigan highlight tape in the Timberwolves' office. Lowe took care of us.

There were just so many high-level games that you hardly had time to appreciate it at the time. We had the two regular-season games with LSU in 1991 and 1992. It was Shaquille O'Neal versus Christian Laettner. Those were unbelievable games, and we won both of them by double digits.

We went to five straight Final Fours when I got to Duke. Are you kidding me? After those five in a row, we got knocked out by Jason Kidd and Cal at Allstate Arena in Chicago in 1993 in the second round. The Final Four was in New Orleans that year, and I had never been there when we weren't working. I'd been a college coach five years and I didn't know what to do at the convention because we'd always been playing. Amaker didn't either, so we flew to New Orleans together and we got to the Hilton, and there were people everywhere in the lobby. We checked in, and Eddie Fogler, who played and coached under Dean Smith at North Carolina, saw us at the elevator and said, "You guys don't know what the hell to do here, do you?"

We went up to the room and sat around and we said, "What do we do?" I said to Amaker, "Are you hungry?" And he said, "Yeah." So I said, "I think there's a good oyster place right around here."

We went to our oyster place and we were sitting there and we kept asking, "So what's the convention like? What do you do?" Gaudet had been to lots of conventions as a high school coach. We finally called him and said, "Pete, what do you do during the day?"

That's how totally spoiled we were. I'd been a college coach five years and been to five straight Final Fours.

I remember being in Charlotte, getting ready to play the national championship against Arkansas. It was 1994, one of the last times the game was in a regular-sized arena, by the way. I had Arkansas in terms of scouting, and so we went through our notebooks. It was April, 75 degrees, and we'd been inside a gym all winter. So we went to an outdoor court at a high school. Our guys got up in the bleachers at the softball field. I sat on the rail in the bleachers and went over personnel. Mike K just wanted to do something refreshing so we did the walk-through on the blacktop instead of going to the arena just as a way to change it up. That was an amazing memory. We were going over the national championship scouting reports sitting in the bleachers at James Middle School and then going out on the blacktop and walking through their stuff. Scotty Thurman hit the big three-point shot to beat us in that one. I remember Bill Clinton, who was all fired up because he was an Arkansas guy, coming in our locker room afterward. That was pretty cool.

And there always were unbelievable games with Carolina. It was nuts to be so caught up in the Duke-Carolina thing and live it every day. My kids were getting a little older then, especially Kyle. When we lost to Carolina, I mentally prepared him before he went to school because they were on his case. A lot of his teachers were from Carolina, and sometimes it seemed like everybody was a Carolina fan. When Kyle was in kindergarten and first grade, I'd tell him, "Hey, Kyle, be ready, they're coming after you today." And he'd say, "Yeah, I know, Dad, I know." When we beat 'em, I would go to our regular lunch spot, though sometimes we'd pick up lunch at the drive-through to just stay out of there. I take a page out of that book at Notre Dame sometimes. If we lose a couple, I may not go to my breakfast spot at Uptown Kitchen for a couple of days. I'll just do the drive-through at Starbucks. If we win a game, I'll go back to Uptown. It's a crazy way of living, but that's the way it works.

Dean Smith was always so good to me because I was Morgan's guy, even though I was also a Duke guy. On the road or before games, he would say, "How you doing? Mike, you've really got a beautiful family. I was looking at the media guide. How's Morgan?" Coach Smith would always spend time with you. But being in the midst of all that was intense, and then you had Jimmy Valvano at North Carolina State. You were living it every day of the year—even in the offseason while recruiting against Carolina. Every day you were in it. It was just an amazing dynamic down there and it was really an honor to be part of it.

Mike K was so intense back then. After games we would go to his house. It was somebody's rotation to pick up the pizzas, and we would watch the game film. So we'd get to his house about

10:00 or 10:15 after a 7:00 PM game. We'd put the VHS tape in his machine, and he had the clicker. We all had our assigned seats. I always used to kid Amaker because he used to sit up front. We would start the tape. And here goes one play, and Mike K would pause it and say, "What was going on with this guy tonight?" We would go into a psychological discourse on all our guys. Sometimes we would walk out of the house at 2:30 or 3:00 in the morning.

On the road, we didn't do charter flights back then, so we'd stay overnight after the game and we'd go to Mike K's room and watch it. We'd sleep a few hours and then jump on a plane. By the end of the season, you were exhausted. We'd have some 9:00 PM games and then get to his house at maybe 12:30 or 1:00. I can remember leaving the house so late (or early in the morning) that I'd grab the newspaper on the driveway and toss it closer to Mike K's door.

Mike K was a machine. He didn't need sleep; he was unbelievable. Amaker and I would look at each other some days and think, *Well, here we go.* It was intense because you were in the middle of it all the time. You didn't have cell phones in those days or many other distractions, so you were just in the bunker. But it was an unbelievable learning experience because you just were in it every single day. There was pizza every night, and then for a little celebration, Mike K would have ice cream. That was how he would splurge.

At the end of the year, we would get job offers and we didn't have much left. I just wanted to go home for a week with my family and recruit a little bit. I wasn't sure I had the energy to take a job. We were good about picking our spots and getting away a little bit in May. Of course, back then the recruiting period was June 15 to August 1, and you could be out on the road chasing prospects that whole time. No one was out recruiting all six weeks because we were running camps at the same time.

All this was good because no one ever made an unofficial visit in August. Once you got to August 1, you went, "All right, we've got two or three weeks." Mike K would let us use his condo down in Morehead City, North Carolina. We would go down as a family, stay at his condo, and get to the beach a little bit. Then eventually we would drive to Wrightsville Beach, which is only two hours from Durham. And we called the office every day to check in and see what was up.

This is why Mike K was great. He would go on vacation and take all the game film from the previous season to the beach. He'd go down for two weeks, maybe two-and-a-half weeks, after recruiting in August. We'd all go to our places. I went to Ocean City, Maryland, because my parents retired up there. So we'd go up there and visit and then head to Rehoboth Beach because my wife's parents were up there. Mike K would run on the beach, but then he would shut himself in a room and watch games. And he would come back with all kinds of notes on different stuff. We always knew at the first meeting in late August he would come in with a notepad of all this stuff. And that's why we won.

Going into the 1989–90 season, my third year there, Quin Snyder had just graduated, and so Hurley, even though he was only a freshman, had to be the point guard. He's got to be the guy. So Mike K comes back in the office. It's the first meeting, and he has got all kinds of notes. We're really focused on Hurley and talking about what we've got to do with him. Mike K had a lot of points.

It was Jay Bilas' first year with us, maybe his first meeting. He had just started law school and was going to be our graduate assistant coach. And Mike K goes, "What do you think? Is that too much to ask for Bobby?" I said, "Coach, that may be a little much for him. Do we think we can simplify that a little bit?" Mike K came back and said, "I'll tell you one thing: we're gonna do it. You guys that work with the guards are gonna get him there. We can't lower the standard." Mike K had made his point, and it was very intense.

The meeting broke up, and we all went to our offices. About 10 minutes later, Bilas came down the hall and he had this really serious look on his face. He said, "Are all the meetings like that?" And we all broke up. We kept each other loose and sometimes we were able to keep Mike K loose, too. He had a great sense of humor, so when you could get in that mode, we had some fun telling stories and laughing. It was an amazing experience to be part of it, especially because of the intensity of so many of the conference rivalries.

Bilas was really interested in being a coach, and Amaker was offered the USC job by the athletic director there, Mike Garrett, and Amaker was really thinking about it. They danced for about two weeks. Bilas was from Los Angeles, and he was hoping Amaker would take it, so he could become an assistant for the Trojans, but Amaker to USC never happened.

So I always talk to Bilas about how he got with the law firm in Charlotte, started doing Duke games on radio, then did some ACC regional games on television, and the rest is history. He's found a great niche. He misses teaching and coaching, and that's why he has gotten involved with some camps where he works with the big guys. I think that fills a void where he can still coach a little bit.

But this is how smart Mike K is: he gave Bilas the GA job so Bilas could pay for law school, just to take care of him. And Bilas never missed a meeting. He graduated probably in the top 10 percent of his law school class and yet he was at every single basketball event. I used to tell him, "Hey, you don't have to be at everything." He'd say, "I got my stuff straight." He just had everything handled. It was cool having him around. We developed a really close relationship that exists today.

Gaudet was another assistant while I was at Duke, and he and I were joined at the hip because we were both former high school coaches. Mike K liked having guys with high school experience. He would brag about it. Mike K called me the "beer and pizza guy." He'd say, "I've got Amaker who is stealth, and Brey who is the beer and pizza guy. He's out at the bar at night on the road recruiting, and that's where he gets info and feedback." That was his scouting report on us. Bob Knight called everybody by their last names, so Mike K similarly would say, "We turned Brey loose in the Irish bar on the road up at Five-Star Camp. He'll have all the information in two hours. Amaker does it like the CIA."

I wish the last year—1994–95 when we finished 13–18—would have been a really positive year. But it was kind of time for me to do something new. And I think it was probably a good time for Mike K to change things up. And then who replaced me? Snyder, the former Duke player who was ready. Now Mike K's on a run with his former guys—kind of like I am now here at Notre Dame. I have pretty good depth in that department. In the past I've had guys who would call me when I had an opening, but no one calls now because they know what direction I'm going to go.

Now that I'm at Notre Dame, I have to compete against Mike K all the time. But it's been neat, really cool, playing in a lot of big games. We've played in a bunch of those, and Mike K is always so gracious. It was really touching before the ACC Championship Game in 2017. He grabbed me before the game and he said,

"You know, I'm so damn proud of you." I said, "Coach, I'm not anywhere near any of this if not for my experience with you."

He's just been really proud and supportive, even though we're competing against each other now. It makes for an interesting dynamic. The first time playing against Duke was in Greenville, South Carolina, in the NCAA Tournament in 2002 when the Blue Devils were a No. 1 seed. It was crazy because we had Chris Thomas at the line, a 90 percent free-throw shooter, with a one-and-one and a chance to go up seven. He missed, and Daniel Ewing came right back down and hit a three, and we couldn't hold on. Mike K was great there after the game. He was really gracious and proud and said that we played great.

I've always been a really competitive person. I get that from my mother. I have her edge and I guess I have that naturally. And then being around Mike K's laboratory of competing every day, that was really good for me. It was a really good situation for me to develop. Now I get to the offseason and I wish I could turn it off more. But to be successful and to not get fired, you've got to think about your program every day—recruiting, marketing, all the rest. Your mind races with it, but it was great to be around his edge and his fight because, man, he's still got it. I'm a firm believer that he likes to eat his young. There are no charity cases when he's played against his guys historically. He's not letting up, and I respect that.

I really think probably after 2015—after we won the ACC Tournament and we'd had some success against Duke and Carolina—I felt like I had arrived. And now when we talk in the summer, it's two contemporaries. I'm involved with the National Association of Basketball Coaches stuff now; Mike K was heavily involved and was the head of it for a while when I was an assistant with him. So we talk about a lot of big picture issues.

Those were eight years at Duke that flew by because we were so darned busy. We didn't pause enough to enjoy it, and that's part of the reason Mike K wore himself out a little bit. After he won the second one, Mike K never wanted to be a big-time guy. He always wanted to be down to Earth. He wanted everybody to be able to connect with him, so everybody asked him to do stuff, and he said yes to everything. And that wasn't always good. In hindsight he looks back and he's gotten much better at that after the back surgery and the exhaustion. But in the beginning when I was there, he did everything, so we did everything, too.

I remember one time right after we had won it all in 1992. I was in Cameron Indoor Stadium, and somebody was shooting free throws. I was talking with one of the players, and Mike K was coming from a workout that he snuck in for 30 minutes because he had 20 things on his list. It was May after we won the second one, and the banner was already up. And so he came in and sat and watched whoever was shooting free throws. When he left I came up to chat with him, and he was drinking a Gatorade. He looked up at the banner and said, "Man, we haven't taken enough time to enjoy that, have we?"

And I said, "Coach, I don't think we have, and you certainly have not. I know you've got a lot of people pulling at you and I hope you can get some time to get your energy back because we need you."

I was worried about him. I said, "We're gonna need you, man. So I hope you and Mickie can get out of here with the kids and turn the phones off."

And he said, "Yeah, we gotta do that."

I've tried to learn from that. That's one of the reasons I don't come to the office real early sometimes. I like to go to Knollwood

Country Club to get a workout in and clear my head a little bit. Then I get in here later in the morning.

I still talk to a lot of Duke guys—Laettner, Marty Clark. I see Hurley on the road. We tell some stories. Hurley got a kick out of what I said in Buffalo at the 2017 NCAA Tournament about Matt Farrell being better than him. All the reporters called him, of course, and I saw him on the road that summer and said, "Bobby, you know I was just pumping my guy up." He said, "I know, Coach. I'm the one that told you to recruit him."

I went to Delaware for five years, and Mike K would always leave a great voicemail after we won a championship. My third year he left me an unbelievable voicemail—I wish I'd saved it— about being a winner. It was just awesome to hear that from a guy you worked with. When I got the job at Notre Dame, he found me when I was in Cincinnati watching Jordan Cornette. He tracked me down on the cellphone and he said, "Pace yourself. Don't try and do it all the first week. It's a lot to handle, it's a great job, you're perfect for it."

Here's another story he loves to tell. I go to the Nike Camp in Indianapolis on Friday, and that's the day Matt Doherty left Notre Dame for North Carolina. On Saturday at Nike it's already buzzing, and I've got guys bumping me about the Notre Dame situation. I watched the morning games. And Mike K and I would always go to lunch at Palomino, a restaurant right across from the Hyatt in downtown Indianapolis, when I was at Duke. So he called and said, "Let's go to lunch, same place, same table." I came walking to the table, and he was humming the Notre Dame Victory March. He said, "It's over, you're the guy, there's nobody else. It's over, Mike, prepare yourself." He always said one of his guys from Duke should be in that Notre Dame job.

Mike K grew up a big Notre Dame guy in Chicago. Joe Sassano, who helped run the Joyce Center for years, was his football coach at Weber High School. Mike K always had a great affinity for this place, always has been a Notre Dame football guy. If anything had ever happened at Duke way back when, here's a Chicago Catholic League guy who probably would have been a great fit here. He's always watched this place. If you grow up Catholic at Weber High School, you're a Notre Dame guy.

In 1992 we went to the Rose Garden to meet president George H.W. Bush after winning the NCAA title. It was our Duke team and Pat Summitt and the Tennessee women's team. And Digger was there because he was running the Weed and Seed program, a $500 million initiative designed to weed out inner-city drug problems and seed those same neighborhoods with constructive youth programs, for President Bush. Digger sat in the front row, and President Bush introduced him. It made me think of all the Duke guys off that particular team, including Laettner, Hurley, and Billy McCaffery—whom he had recruited while he was at Notre Dame. So ultimately something about Notre Dame seemed to pop up every time I turned around.

I was in Durham for eight years and after about year six I began thinking, *I'm ready, I'd like to become a head coach.* After year eight, which was the year when Mike K was out, Delaware became just the perfect situation. But after going from high school to Duke University, over those eight years, I was there for an unbelievable run.

The Delaware Years

THEY USED TO TEASE TOMMY AMAKER AND ME ALL THE TIME. Other guys out there in the profession would say to both of us, "How can you not be interested in interviewing for that job?"

But as Tommy and I used to talk about all the time, we were on that Final Four run at Duke, so we were coaching right up through the first few days of April. By the time the season ended, we were so exhausted. To jump into a new thing, we had nothing left.

I remember hearing it from Perry Clark, a good friend who coached me at DeMatha and later was the head coach at Tulane and Miami (Florida). He used to grab Tommy and me and say, "Who do you guys think you are, turning jobs down? You know how many people would like those?"

But we were young. In a lot of situations, I just felt like I didn't have enough juice to do it. The job I really wanted and couldn't get was the Vanderbilt job. Eddie Fogler, the Commodores' former coach, was going to South Carolina and he was trying to help me. They ended up hiring Jan van Breda Koff, who was a former player and also had head coaching experience at Cornell. I just thought the academic fit would have been good there, and there were just a lot of other things I liked about the program.

I was in the mix for jobs at North Carolina-Wilmington, Baylor, and Saint Louis over a couple of different years. I met with a lot of people through the years. I was offered the Auburn job. I really thought, *Hey, it's an SEC job, you got to do it.* That was an interesting one because we won the regional in 1994 against Glenn Robinson and Purdue and then went to the Final Four in Charlotte. Instead of going back with Duke to get ready for the Final Four, I flew to Auburn. I met with the president and the athletic director. They made the call and offered me the job, and I said, "You know I really feel good about it, but I would like to finish our season at Duke."

I got back to Durham Sunday, and we were getting ready to play Florida in Charlotte the next Saturday in the semifinals of the Final Four. Now it just so happened the Auburn president was in Raleigh on some kind of committee. He said, "Come over and let's meet tomorrow." So I drove over and sat with him at his hotel. He hadn't been real involved when I was on campus. But I think he felt he was going for the jugular here. I had a great meeting with him, I really liked him and I told him I felt really good about it. I said, "Let's just sit on it and let me get through the weekend."

By the time I got home—back when there were no cell phones—my wife, Tish said, "Well, you must have taken it. I've had eight calls."

I said, "What are you talking about?"

I think the president got on the horn right away with the people back at Auburn and said, "He's coming. We got him." So now it was out there.

We went through a couple more days, and I was on the bus with the team headed to Charlotte. Mike Krzyzewski said, "Come up and sit with me" because he could tell I wasn't sure what to do. We sat together for about an hour of the three-hour ride from

Durham to Charlotte. We talked a lot about the fit. I kept thinking about coaching in the SEC.

But I got off the bus at the Embassy Suites, and there was a pep rally going on, and people were everywhere. I walked in, went right to my room, and called the Auburn athletic director, David Housel. We kid about this now, but I said, "David, I'm just not the guy, and you need to know that now."

Cliff Ellis really wanted the job. He had just been let go at Clemson and was working Mike K to help him, and I was in the way. So I got out of it, and then the Auburn people were worried about which booster got involved, and I said, "Nobody did that. I'm telling you I just don't think I'm a great fit for you. I'm flattered and I'm honored. And don't worry, I won't say I was offered the job. I don't need to say I was offered the job. I'm good."

Ellis was hired three days later, and I went back to Duke for another year.

Delaware's courtship was very unusual because that's the year Mike K went out with a bad back and exhaustion. And we were struggling. We were really young. Steve Wojciechowski was a freshman, and so was Trajan Langdon. Everyone we played wanted to get their shots in when we were down.

We were at the Greensboro Marriott that year for the ACC Tournament. C.M. Newton, the former Vanderbilt coach, tracked me down. I'd gotten to know him because he was on the NCAA Basketball Committee and I represented Duke at meetings while I was there. He always seemed to kind of take a liking to me. He took me under his wing and mentored me a little bit.

C.M. said to me, "A very good friend of mine is the president at the University of Delaware. And he'd be very interested in talking to you about their basketball job."

I said, "Coach, do you think that's a good job for me?"

He said, "I think it's a great job for you because Dave Roselle is the best president to have if you're a basketball coach."

Now Mike K was not in the picture. He was a little removed because of his health issues, so there was not really anybody to talk to. I was kind of flying here and there and I'm thinking, *You know, it's eight years, it's probably time.* By now the season had ended, so I met with Delaware initially, and it was clear that Roselle was making the hire. He really made me feel I was their guy.

Delaware had an arena—the Bob Carpenter Center—that was fairly new. It was in the mid-Atlantic so I knew the high school coaches in the area. So I was thinking maybe this would be a good fit. Then Mike K came back in April, and we were on the road recruiting. In fairness to him, he didn't really want any changes in his staff after being out that year. He was really on me about, "Don't sell yourself short. Maybe you can do better than Delaware." But I just thought it was a great fit, and it was time. Those eight years there had been unbelievable, but it was time to do it.

A lot of people might wonder, *How can you turn down an SEC job and then take Delaware the next year?* The younger, ambitious guys would say to me, "I can't believe you would do that. That's a difference of a couple $100,000." But the guys whose opinions I really valued said, "Really smart move. You're going to a place in your region, you can learn to coach, you have a little bit more control of the situation, you're not thrown into the SEC."

I accepted the Delaware job, and it really did work out for me because I was able to make my mistakes—but not on national television. There was less pressure, fewer people in the gym. I had unbelievable support from David Roselle, the Delaware president. Though we got going a little bit late, we were able to put together a bit of a recruiting class. We were a little bit in scramble mode in recruiting, but we got a good guard out of Newport News, Virginia, by the name of Tyrone Perry. And we got a couple of transfers and we started to build it.

Sean Kearney had been at Delaware as an assistant with the previous coach, and I kept him because he just knew where everything was. He really became a great right-hand man. In fact, I kept both the full-time assistants. In those days it's not like you were paying big money and could just go out and get any guy you wanted to hire. Kearney was unbelievable administratively, which you needed at a mid-major program because you don't have as much help.

The other assistant was Darryl Bruce, who was a DeMatha guy I actually had in my history class. Then I brought a former Duke student manager, Jeff LaMere, as my restricted earnings coach, and then Mike K took him away from me back to Duke a year later. That was our staff, and it was just perfect.

It was neat because we were in a great spot in that region. We'd been in the south a little bit in Durham, and we loved it, but at Delaware you were a two-hour drive from everywhere— New York City, Philadelphia, New Jersey, Baltimore, and D.C. I would get in my car and drive two hours and see all the players we needed to see. We were right on I-95, the Carpenter Center was new, and it was easy to pull off and see it.

Then, talk about timing. Before the school hired me, Delaware agreed to host all the rounds except the championship of the America East Tournament. So for five years, we had all the preliminary rounds of our conference tournament in our own building. As much as other coaches may have complained about it, we were the only ones really selling tickets, so the other athletic directors couldn't move it somewhere else. The good part was we had the games at home; the bad part was that you better do well if you're the host. And in my first two years, we got knocked out in the first round. Then in years three and four, we won it before losing in the title game in year five.

Delaware was the right move because I was confident there. What helped me was that there were all those high school coaches who I knew in that area. When I was an assistant at Duke, I had been good to them when they came down to the clinic or needed tickets. Now I wanted to recruit their guys, and they were like, "Hey, Mike took care of us. We're gonna help him." So there were lots of continuing relationships, a lot of deep relationships.

We went to DeMatha and got two guys—Darryl Presley and Mike Pegues—who became the starting front line of my championship teams. Presley was a transfer from Virginia that we picked him off, and Pegues came right out of high school. We were hitting Baltimore, we were going into Philly, we were going to Jersey.

Morgan Wootten was coaching my guy, Pegues, who was a bit heavy, maybe a little overweight, but really skilled around the bucket. Virginia Tech and Marquette were intrigued about him, but the Virginia Tech assistants could never convince the head coach into taking him so they fell off. Marquette missed on somebody, so they were still in it. I was close to getting a commitment from Mike. And I'd been recruiting him by myself; nobody else on our staff was talking to him. I had the whole school at DeMatha helping me. It was like, "Mike gets this one." I had a home visit with Mike and his mother and I was driving back from Maryland to Delaware. I called Coach Wootten and I said, "Coach, great news. Mike committed. He's gonna sign next week with us."

Coach said, "Well, that's great, Mike. This message I have from Marquette I can just throw away, I guess."

I said, "Yeah, Coach, if you could throw that message away that would be great."

And Pegues became the all-time leading scorer at Delaware and was the linchpin that we played around. He was the Bonzie Colson of those teams and he's now an assistant coach at Louisville.

Many times I would look down the hall and see our football coach at Delaware, Tubby Raymond. Tubby had been there 30 years, and I understood why. It was a great lifestyle. My kids would jump in the car with me, and Rehoboth Beach was 70 miles away. We bought a place there, and I always thought, *This is pretty good here. I'm driving everywhere to recruit, I'm not on a plane.* And how strange was it that the day Tubby died in 2017, I was coaching Notre Dame, and my team was back there to play Delaware. Being out on the floor during the moment of silence was really poignant.

I was 30–28 after my second year at Delaware. Coming from Duke, I came in there with a lot of hype and then I was on the hot seat in year three. I thought to myself, *You come with the background from Duke, and there are people thinking you have this magic wand and that the process is quicker than it really is.* So it was a blessing and a curse with all the success we had in Durham. Fortunately, we won the America East title in years three and four, and now we were selling the building out and we had it going. But I recognized I was being held to a little bit different standard. That comes with the territory and so you better be ready.

I never ever remember being so mentally exhausted as at the end of that second season at Delaware. Your mind races with every detail for the five-month season. Even when you're sleeping, you're dreaming about the stuff you were thinking about before you went to bed. I remember being flat-out exhausted at the end because you just were on it. As a young coach you don't know how to pace yourself as much. Sometimes you need time for a workout to clear your head. I was just rolling all the time, on it all the time, and thinking about it all the time.

My son, Kyle, tells stories about how he and I would go to Christiana Mall in Newark, Delaware. He says, "Dad, you and I would be walking around, you'd get a cell call, and I'm four years old. And you'd walk out into the mezzanine to take the call, and, Dad, I'm only four! I'm left in the store by myself. I'm looking around. Dad? *Dad*?"

Meanwhile, I'm out near the Starbucks somewhere telling someone, "Yeah, Delaware would be a great spot for you." Then I'm thinking, *Oh, crap, where's Kyle?* So it's not always great for your family.

My daughter Callie was always great about people coming to our table when she was 12. She was very protective of that both at Delaware—and especially here at Notre Dame. She'd say, "Excuse me, we're having a family dinner." And, of course, when a 12-year-old does that, guys run the other way.

In our third year in 1997–98, we kind of kicked it into gear and went 20–10. We were probably a year ahead of schedule and we were able to go to the NCAA Tournament. We played in Chicago, and Purdue beat us 95–56. I remember telling one of the officials, Mike Kitts, in the second half when we were out of timeouts, "Mike, if any of my guys call timeout jumping out of bounds, I hope you would ignore it." He said, "I got you, Coach." And then I jokingly said, "Any chance we could go to a running clock?" He said, "Yeah, I feel you, Coach, but I can't do that."

But no one celebrated more after an NCAA Tournament loss. When you're a No. 15 seed and it's the first time you get in, you're gonna enjoy it. We stayed at the Palmer House and we had a heck of a reception after the game. You would have thought we threw one in at the buzzer against Purdue when we actually got beat by almost 40. But we got there.

For those Delaware teams to get there—and they had been in the NCAA Tournament back-to-back years in 1991 and 1992—was a source of pride. When we got back there, that meant Delaware went four times in the 1990s, and that's pretty good.

The next year in 1998–99 we were the top of the league and got the No. 13 seed in the bracket. We had Tennessee on the ropes in Charlotte in the NCAA first round and just couldn't finish it in a 62–52 loss. That was one where we were disappointed because we thought we were primed for an upset.

We came back in year five in 1999–2000 and still had a good group, but it was kind of a changing of the guard. Jay Wright at Hofstra was starting to build it there. He had a guard by the name of Speedy Claxton, who played in the NBA for about a decade. We lost to them in the America East championship game at Hofstra. We got to the NIT, though, which was a big step for a second team to get in the NIT from our league. We lost at Villanova in the NIT, and little did I know that would be my last year at Delaware, even though it didn't happen until July.

I'll never forget getting on the bus after we lost at Hofstra. We're coming down from Long Island after playing in three straight America East championship games. I remember thinking to myself, *Maybe it's time for the next challenge. You may have maxed out here.* I felt that even more so after we lost to Villanova a week later in the NIT.

I got great advice on being a head coach from Mike K and Morgan. I worked for two very strong personalities. But you've gotta be yourself, you gotta find your own personality. As far as the style of how I interacted, I was always very conscious to kind of find myself as soon as I could. That's hard to do when you're not the most confident head coach and you haven't really done anything yet.

One of the things I think you learn to do as you become more experienced—and I did it later in my years at Delaware—is to be a better delegator. When I got the job, I felt like I had to do everything. I remember Kearney coming to me once the second year and saying, "Are you gonna let me help you with recruiting at all?"

I was just a buzz saw. I was just on everything—no different than when I was an assistant. I think as I got more trusting, got to know Kearney and Bruce, got it going a little bit after the third year when we had some momentum, then I was better at delegating. I was more secure as a head coach, I was able to show my personality more to the team. I could be loose with them some days and not worry about them thinking it wasn't business. I got more confident after that third year, and then we won the conference championship in the third and fourth years. Then you start to feel like we've got a pretty good culture here and have figured out how to do this thing.

Through it all the biggest thing was just relationships with the guys. That was the high school teacher and coach in me. You go to the dorms, you're involved with everything, you talk to everybody, and so you became visible on campus. You're always selling. I was always trying to market the program. There was this really hot band called Love Seed Mama Jump, and they still play at the beach in Delaware. We had just won the league title and we

My family—Shane, Paul, and me (back row) and Betty and Brenda (front row)—pose for a photo. (Mike Brey)

Morgan Wootten, my longtime mentor, is to my left as I coach DeMatha Catholic High, where I played and coached under him. (Mike Brey)

I was all about sports growing up. (Mike Brey)

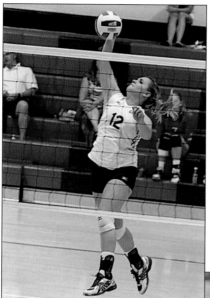

My daughter, Callie, is the one who convinced me to adopt my open-collar look. (Tish Brey)

My son, Kyle, played at University of Buffalo before moving on to a career coaching football. (Tish Brey)

I learned a lot while coaching under Mike Krzyzewski from 1987 to 1995, including how hard you need to compete every day. (Mike Brey)

I console Mike Pegues after we lost to Tennessee in the 1999 NCAA Tournament. That was a tough loss, but I loved coaching at Delaware from 1995 to 2000. (AP Images)

I speak at the July 2000 press conference that announced my hiring as Notre Dame basketball coach. It was a dream come true. (Lighthouse Imaging)

The team presents me with the commemorative gameball in November of 2000 after I won my first game at Notre Dame and 100th career victory. (Lighthouse Imaging)

Ryan Humphrey, who is now an assistant coach with me, throws down a dunk during our win against Xavier in 2001, which was my first NCAA Tournament victory at Notre Dame. (AP Images)

I coach our squad during the 2002–03 season, when we went 24–10 and reached the Sweet 16. (Lighthouse Imaging)

Dan Miller (left) and Matt Carroll celebrate our NCAA Tournament win against Illinois in 2003. Miller, who led us with 23 points in that game, used to kid me about being the only player who got us to the second weekend of the Tournament. (AP Images)

I coach our team in 2003–04, a year in which we went 9–7 in the Big East and 19–13 overall. (Lighthouse Imaging)

Off the court, I love the experience of being on Notre Dame's campus, which was captured during this photo from the 2003–04 season. (Heather Gollatz-Dukeman)

Chris Quinn, the first Notre Dame player I signed, displays his intensity during a double-overtime game against Georgetown in 2006. (AP Images)

I'm so glad that Kyle McAlarney, who handles the ball during a 2008 win against Syracuse when he made nine three-pointers, rejoined our team. (AP Images)

Luke Harangody, who was three-time All-Big East for us and one of the best players I've ever coached, dunks in 2008. (AP Images)

Syracuse head coach Jim Boeheim and I have remained friendly while battling in the Big East and ACC and working together on the National Association of Basketball Coaches. (*USA TODAY* Sports Images)

The Notre Dame student section starts to storm the court after we defeated eventual national champion Louisville in five overtimes in 2013. (*USA TODAY* Sports Images)

were starting to create some buzz. I had met the lead singer one summer and I tracked down his number. They were playing at this bar called the Big Kahuna in Wilmington, Delaware, out on the water. Everybody in the athletic department was going, and I'm thinking to myself, *I've got to get a Delaware jersey on the lead singer*. I was my own PR guy.

I tracked the guy down and I said, "I'm just asking you a favor." I went up there while they were rehearsing and I came in with the jersey. I said, "Look, you don't know me very well."

And he said, "Hey, Coach, I know you, you've had a good year." They were from Dewey Beach, so they followed us a little bit. He said, "Coach, I know you got it going a little bit."

I said, "Man, most of UD will be up here tonight. Could you just do the opening set in Kestutis Marciulionus' jersey?"

He said, "No problem, Coach."

The next day I had 20 people from the department come in and tell me, "Mike, you wouldn't believe it. The star of the band had Marciulionus' jersey on."

I played dumb. I said, "Are you kidding me?"

I said, "I guess we're catching on."

There is a magazine called *Delaware Today*, and they have a "best of the state" section in the summer. We were in the running for best sports team because we had just won our second league championship. So I got hold of the editor. I wore him out for three weeks. I told him, "We need to be the cover."

I had a guard, John Gordon, who was from Saint Mark's High School in Newark, Delaware. He had transferred in from Maine. He was a hero when we got him back and a really good player. I said, "John Gordon and I should be the cover." We finally got it done, and on the cover, I'm holding a plate of the "best of" nachos, and John is in his uniform reaching over my shoulder.

When I first got the Delaware job and tried to get the camp going, I'd have Grant Hill and Bobby Hurley come and speak. When those guys came to camp, we would get 50 more campers. The media was there talking about basketball, and we had the buzz.

I was the marketing guy every day, thinking, *How do we get out there? How do we push it?* Football would get 30,000 fans in that stadium every Saturday. We had to able to get 4,000. Delaware is a small state so you had a platform to get out there. Joe Biden was at a lot of our games, and it seemed like everybody knew everybody in this little state.

We lived right in Newark, Delaware. It's a great town, and you had Wilmington to the north. We loved the beach and we were 77 miles from our beach house. So, in the summer, I would work at the beach house, come back for a staff meeting in the morning, and then go back to the beach. It was really kind of cool. I was marketing at the beach. I would walk into restaurants, meet people, and talk about our program. I was selling tickets and I was visible.

It was set up for me in a lot of ways at Delaware because they really gave me every chance to be successful. I told David exactly that when we played back there in December 2017.

We had three Senegalese kids from West Africa on my team, and that was interesting because they spoke a different language in the locker room. We had a Lithuanian guard. I had Gordon, who could have been the governor of Delaware. I had the two DeMatha guys. I had Danny Miller's older brother, Greg, who is a coach now. I had a really unique group. They were really good players, great guys—and they had unique personalities and characters that helped sell the program.

In my fourth year, Jay Bilas had a day off from broadcasting so he came down to watch us practice when we were getting ready for our conference championship game. We had won in the semifinals the week before, and back then you waited a week to play the championship game. Our title game was at 11:00 AM before the ACC semifinals when they were played on Saturdays. In the midst of our practice, Bilas got a phone call. Nancy Lieberman, who was supposed to call our game, had the flu and laryngitis. They said, "Bilas, can you do the game?" So he told his producer, "You won't believe this, but I'm sitting at Delaware's practice right now."

Bilas stayed and did the championship game, and there's a great picture of him interviewing me after the game. In that same photo, one of the students on the side is holding a sign with the saying the kids loved, "Ass-Kickin' Chicken." That's probably the first time Bilas saw a little bit of our looseness. Our team had won it the year before. So this time the biggest thing I was trying to do was keep them loose.

We were watching some film of Drexel after the pregame meal. Bilas was there with us, and I purposely had Kearney pop in the scene where they talk about running the picket fence in the movie *Hoosiers*. Our guys are like, "Holy crap." Bilas said, "You've got to be kidding? You're playing for the title tomorrow." I said, "Gotta keep 'em loose, man. Gotta keep 'em loose." At first my time at Delaware was different because I had not been a head coach. I hadn't learned how to compartmentalize as much. I needed to say, "Okay, put the job stuff over there." I was just trying not to get fired. Certainly getting to the NCAA Tournament in year three was key at Delaware. I was the co-coach of the year in the league with Tom Brennan, so I started saying, "Okay, we can breathe a little bit here. Maybe we can do this." But when you really sat back and looked at it, I really had to deliver. So you were on it every day, your mind's racing, and you were thinking about it all the time. But I wouldn't have had it any other way.

It was a charmed life at Delaware. There were a lot of good people there. You had a lot of people who wanted you to do well. I was fortunate. If you were just good to people and talked to them, there were a lot people who wanted to root for you. Because it was smaller, I could have my own little world. It was really simple because I lived five minutes from our arena. I'd drive up and down I-95 to recruit, and drive down Route 1 to the beach. That was my world. In a way I was kind of in a little bubble that was really cool. It was really kind of refreshing and healthy. Our kids loved it; summers were great. Kyle sometimes would ride with me in the car to go watch games in D.C.

My dilemma was going to come when Kyle was ready to go to high school. Whether we sent him to Saint Mark's or Salesianum, the other school was going to be upset. They were working me hard, and I kind of dodged a bullet by taking the Notre Dame job.

When Kyle was 12, he went to the Duke golf camp with some of our old neighbors from Durham. It turned out Mike Johnston, the former Notre Dame kicker, lived in our neighborhood back when I was coaching at Duke. We became family friends. So we sent Kyle down, and he was going to stay with Mike and his family, and then Mike was going to take them to golf camp the next day. Kyle was having a great time playing golf. Meanwhile, I'm in the midst of this whole thing with the Notre Dame opening. My parents were going to pick him up because I couldn't get him, and my dad wanted to watch the last day of camp and then bring them back. So the Notre Dame thing was going on, we were in the midst of it, and this time Kyle didn't call home.

So Mike went over to pick them up from camp, and I was just about to take the job in South Bend. We'd not had great communication with Kyle while he was at camp, but the rumor is out, and Mike's a Notre Dame guy, so he asked, "Kyle, is your dad going to take the Notre Dame job?" And Kyle said, "Oh, no, my dad just did an extension at Delaware. He's not going anywhere. He's gonna stay at Delaware." That was at 6:00 PM.

At 11:00 that same night, Kyle got a phone call from Tish, and she said, "Your grandparents are going to pick you up tomorrow. Your dad took the Notre Dame job, you'll be here by 2:00, we're leaving at 3:00." Click. That's all he got. As Kyle says now, "I'm sitting there in the neighbors' house and I guess I'm moving." And Mike, of all people, kept going, "You sure your dad's not going to Notre Dame?" So that was a situation where Kyle always says, "Yeah, I'm the last guy to know."

Coming to Notre Dame, Finally

I BECAME INVOLVED WITH THE NOTRE DAME MEN'S BASKETBALL coaching job the first time after they decided to make a change from John MacLeod in 1999. Associate athletics director Bubba Cunningham was handling most of it. Athletics director Mike Wadsworth was the point man, but Bubba was the basketball expert. They called, and, obviously, I was very interested.

The first interview was at the Waldorf-Astoria Hotel in New York. I took the train from Newark, Delaware, up to New York. As I'm walking into Wadsworth's suite, his wife, Bernie, was there with him, and Bubba was kind of running the details. Skip Prosser, the Xavier coach, was walking out, and we shook hands in the hallway. I was there for about two hours, got back on the train, and went back down to Delaware.

At that same time, I was also involved with the Georgia head coaching job. So the next day I flew to Atlanta and I met Vince Dooley, the Georgia athletics director and former football coach, in the Delta Crown Room in the Atlanta airport.

I was still involved with those two, and the NCAA Final Four that year was in Tampa, Florida. The second interview with Notre Dame was at the office of Vince Naimoli, a Notre Dame alumnus and benefactor who was with the Tampa Bay Devil Rays. I also interviewed with Georgia a second time. Then I met with Notre Dame again; this time it was with the president, Rev.

Edward "Monk" Malloy; Lou Nanni, Notre Dame's vice president for university relations; and Wadsworth again. But Bubba was running the show. He was the basketball guy, and you could tell Wadsworth was deferring to him, allowing Bubba to coach him up on the basketball parts. That came on the Friday, the day before the national semifinals.

I met with Georgia again and—in a complete coincidence—I ran into Dooley and Michael Adams, the Georgia president, because they just happened to be sitting four rows in front of me at the semifinal games. They came up to me at halftime of the first game and said, "Hey, we'd love you to be our coach at Georgia and we want to talk to you tomorrow morning." They offered me the job right there in the building. Meanwhile, I still didn't know what was going on with Notre Dame; I hadn't heard any feedback. I met with Georgia the next morning. They told me, "We've got the plane right here on the tarmac, so why don't you go back and pack because we're going to take you to Athens right now?"

Dooley knew I was still involved with Notre Dame, and he's Catholic, so I'm pretty certain he understood the pull and the connection here. I said, "You know I'm really interested, but I'm not really ready to get on a plane right now and do this."

I had the sense I was Dooley's guy. But Adams was visibly upset, and so there was some major tension in the room. I left the meeting, and Dooley walked me down to the car and he said, "Don't worry." Adams was upset because I wouldn't take it right away, and his preference tuned out to be Jim Harrick because they'd been at Pepperdine together. Dooley walked me to the door and said, "Let me give you a ride, Coach."

I said, "You know I'm still interested."

He said, "I know you've got the Notre Dame thing going, but hang in there with us, we'll be all right."

I said, "Okay, just keep me posted."

I found out pretty quickly Adams then offered the job to Harrick. He was their guy. So the Georgia job was gone—and that was actually okay. I was never super anxious about it because I had a good team coming back at Delaware. So it wasn't like, "I've got to get out now."

Then on Monday of the championship game, Wadsworth called me and said, "Mike, we appreciate your interest, but we're going in another direction."

I said, "Mike, thank you, I really appreciate the opportunity."

Nobody had any idea what was going on with Notre Dame. The great scene was the bar at the coaches' hotel after the national championship game Monday night. Connecticut had beaten Duke. Skip Prosser, Gonzaga coach Dan Monson, and I were all there. We were all candidates for the Notre Dame job. Don Monson, a former head coach at Idaho and Oregon and Dan's dad, was there, too. The four of us were there, and Prosser and I look around at the whole group. "You didn't get it? You didn't get it? You didn't get it?" And Don was really giving it to all of us. He said, "Obviously, you guys really did a great job in the interviews."

We're all looking at each other, going, "Well, who got the job if you didn't get it? I didn't get it. You didn't get it." By the next morning, we found out it was Kansas assistant coach and former North Carolina player Matt Doherty. The Notre Dame people really kept that quiet; they did a great job of keeping their decision under wraps.

I thought to myself, *Okay, Georgia's gone, Notre Dame's gone. We're going back to Delaware and we'll be all right because we've got a good team.* My name had definitely been out there, but our fanbase at Delaware was great. They were like, "Hey, just let us know what's going on."

The amazing thing is that the Georgia part wasn't over. I got home from Tampa on Tuesday. I got a call from Dick Bestwick, the assistant athletic director who was handling the Georgia situation. He said, "Mike, do you believe God works in mysterious ways?" Bestwick was a really good guy, a former football coach, and he was doing the legwork for Dooley. He said to me, "Jim Harrick changed his mind."

I said, "You know, Coach Bestwick, I don't think your president is too high on me."

He said, "He would walk to Newark, Delaware, right now. Just think about it and call me back in an hour."

At that point I was just trying to get off the phone because we'd done a radio show back home and I'd already told all the people at Delaware that I was coming back. Bestwick wanted me to call the president's office because that's where all the Georgia people were together meeting. I called his assistant, and she said, "Coach, I'm supposed to patch you right through to the president."

I said, "If you patch me through, I am absolutely hanging the phone up. Please give Dr. Adams a message. I am honored, but I'm going to stay at Delaware. I've told everybody."

It got even more crazy. Within another 24 hours, Harrick changed his mind, came back, and took the job after all. Still, I was comfortable after the Notre Dame and Georgia opportunities didn't happen. My thought was: we've won two league championships, I've got a good group coming back, we're probably going to be competitive again, and we just got to the league championship game again.

Then after my fifth year at Delaware, the Notre Dame situation came around again. It started June 30 when Bill Guthridge resigned at North Carolina. His last season in Chapel Hill had been a little bit of a struggle. The Tar Heels lost 13 games during the regular season, but they did end up getting to the Final Four. I wasn't really following the Carolina search. It was in July, a day before I was headed out on the road. I was headed to the Nike camp in Indianapolis as the Delaware coach. Then I read on the ESPN scroll, "Roy Williams changes his mind, will not go to North Carolina." So he was not going to leave Kansas like most people had expected.

I was at our beach house in Rehoboth Beach on Friday, July 7, and picked up a copy of *USA TODAY* and was reading about Williams deciding to stay in Lawrence, Kansas. Now I was starting to do the math. I turned to my son, Kyle, and I said, "You may think I'm crazy, but we may need to get ready for South Bend again."

I was thinking Doherty had to be the next guy on the Carolina list. He was family, and I wasn't sure there was anyone else. That was Friday. Then on Saturday I walked into the Nike event in Indianapolis. Clark came right up to me and said, "You're interested, right?" I knew he was talking about Notre Dame.

I said, "Absolutely, nothing's changed."

It was amazing. There were just so many people bumping me—all kinds of people connected to Kevin White, Notre Dame's athletic director at the time—that I had to leave the camp. I said, "I've got to get out of here." It got so crazy that I couldn't evaluate anything when it came to players. I just flew back to Delaware, and then on Monday, Missy Conboy, the Notre Dame senior associate athletics director, called. I always used to tease her because her call was kind of like, "Well, I'm not sure if you'd be interested again." This was right when Kevin had started as athletic director at Notre Dame; he'd been on the job about a month.

On Friday afternoon—the seventh of July—the city of South Bend already had planned on hosting a big reception downtown at the College Football Hall of Fame as a welcome for Kevin and Jane White. So all the movers and shakers in all different areas of the community were there to meet Kevin and Jane for the first time. But by then Kevin knew that Matt was already on a plane headed for Chapel Hill and was not coming back. So Kevin couldn't wait to finish that event because he needed to get on a plane himself to start finding another coach.

I wasn't a part of any of that quite yet because the first thing Kevin had to do was fly to Europe that Friday. That was because Big East Conference commissioner Mike Tranghese was really pushing P.J. Carlesimo, the former Seton Hall, Portland Trail Blazers, and Golden State Warriors coach, for the Notre Dame job. Carlesimo was actually on his honeymoon on a boat someplace, and that's where Kevin went. We all laugh about it now. When I saw Carlesimo later down the road, he said, "You know you're the right guy for that."

Anyhow, Conboy got me on the phone, and I said, "Nothing's changed. I really think I'm a great fit there, so tell me what I need to do." On Friday the seventh, I made that comment to Kyle, the recruiting period started the eighth, and Doherty officially took the Carolina job three days later. Conboy called again, and this time everybody from the university was in Washington, D.C., because former Notre Dame president Father Theodore Hesburgh was receiving the Congressional Gold Medal. So all the Notre Dame powerbrokers were in D.C. for that presentation.

Conboy said, "Can you drive down Thursday to meet?"

I said, "Absolutely."

Morgan Wootten was obviously a great mentor and adviser for me. I called him on my way back from one of the Notre Dame interviews, and Coach Wootten, being the ultimate diplomat, always would say, "I never tell my players who to marry or where to go to school."

I said, "Coach, I think I've got to take this one if they offer me the job."

And this is as much as he would reveal. He said, "Mike, there's only one Notre Dame."

I think vicariously he's lived a little bit of this through me and certainly because of my connection to DeMatha and D.C. There were so many natural connections. Monk Malloy, the Notre Dame president, even played basketball at Carroll High School.

I went to the Jones Day law offices of Pat McCartan, the chairman of the Notre Dame Board of Trustees. The first question was great because it came from Monk, and he absolutely knows his basketball. He looked at me and said, "How would you use Troy Murphy?" That was great. That's a basketball president and that was the first question, so I outlined my thought on how I wanted to use Murphy. We met as a big group, and I'd met previously with Kevin before one on one. At least three times, Kevin asked, "Now, if we offer you the job, you're going take it?"

I said, "I'm taking the job."

We didn't talk numbers, but I knew it was going to be better than where I was at Delaware. I also knew Ernie Kent, the Oregon head coach, was coming in right after me. Lou wanted to walk me back to the hotel, even though it was right around the corner. He said, "Hey, do you need any directions to get out of here?"

I said, "Hey, Lou, this is my town."

And he said, "Oh, geez, I'm trying to tell Mike how to get out of here, and I completely forgot he's a D.C. guy." We still laugh about that.

So I headed back to Newark, about a two-hour drive. The phone rang about 11:00 that same night. It was Kevin. He again said, "Now, if we offer you the job, you're going to take it? We'd love you to be the coach at Notre Dame."

I said, "I am absolutely honored. What do I need to do?"

He said, "The plane will be there at 9:00 AM tomorrow."

I said, "Kevin, I need some time to talk to my team and my president."

He said, "Okay, 11:00 AM."

I got up early after not sleeping much. We had a couple of our players in summer school, and I found them. There were some tough phone calls. I had an incoming guard by the name of Austin Roland, who is now an assistant coach. He was so emotional. You talk about hanging the phone up and feeling bad. I had a great recruiting class coming—five kids I never ended up coaching.

I went over and talked to my president, David Roselle. He was really great, just so very supportive. I'd actually signed a contract extension on the first of the month to stay at Delaware. Roselle was later quoted in *Sports Illustrated* saying, "I had an agreement with Mike that if one of the majors wanted to hire him and it was a good school, I would help. He did well by us, and we did well by him."

I got to the New Castle Airport in Wilmington, and Notre Dame sent the plane owned by Jim Morse, a former Notre Dame football player and benefactor. Mike Harkins—the Delaware secretary of state, a mover and shaker in the state, and a big basketball guy—was out on the tarmac. I came walking out, and he was talking to the pilots. It was a little bit of an emotional scene, and he said, "I understand, man. It's a great opportunity for you." Then he said to the two pilots, "Do you know where you're taking him when you land?"

Now, remember, these aren't the Notre Dame pilots from South Bend. They said, "We're just getting him to South Bend. We don't know from there."

And Harkins said to them, "You know what, if there's no one there to pick him up, bring his [butt] back."

I was getting on the plane and I'm thinking, *Are we really doing this?* We were just rolling. That was the 14th of July, and that was one week after the day on my porch when I turned to Kyle and said that we had better be ready.

We did the Notre Dame press conference right there on the arena floor of the Joyce Center, and I actually wore a tie that day. But I had walked into the back of the building in my shorts because I wanted to meet with the team. We did that before the press conference, and I wanted to be relaxed so we all just sat in the players' lounge in the locker room right off the court.

My biggest theme with the team was that I knew they were really good, they were really close to getting an NCAA bid the year before. I told them, "I know you guys want to play in the NCAA Tournament. You've got really good players here. I need to learn about you. You guys had a heck of a year, probably should have gotten in the tournament. I just think I can help you with that, so I look forward to working together with you." I felt really comfortable with all of them that day.

When I look back, I didn't really know my bearings when I walked in that back gate of the Joyce Center. The training room was just to the right. I know that now, but I didn't know where anything was that first day. Everything was spinning, everything was a whirlwind. But something caught me out of the corner of my right eye. (I'd been to South Bend one other time to play a game when I was at Duke. All I knew was the Marriott downtown.) But for whatever reason, I took a glance into the training room, and there was Digger Phelps working out on the Stairmaster. It was only fitting that the first person I ran into in South Bend was Digger.

So I walked in, and he said, "Congratulations." Then he said, "Hey, you've got to live in South Bend. Don't live in Granger; you need to live downtown." He was coaching me right away.

I said, "I appreciate that, Coach. There are a lot of things I've got to learn. I really look forward to working with you. I need your advice."

Sports Illustrated ran a long article titled "Domino Effect: Bill Guthridge's Resignation as North Carolina's Coach Set Off a Chain Reaction That Changed the Lives of Scores of People in the Game" in an early September issue on all the things that transpired after Bill resigned. The piece was really amazing because it documented how many coaching situations were affected. A lot of people assumed Ray would go back to Chapel Hill from Kansas, and Matt would end up back at Kansas as head coach. But that's not the way it played out. They quoted me in *Sports Illustrated* saying, "Who'd have thought that all the Carolina movement would help a guy who coached at Duke?"

Then they quoted Matt saying to me, "Want to buy a house?"

After I'd been on campus about a month, I had my first meeting with Monk back in South Bend. I went over to the Main Building, sat down with Monk, and talked through all kinds of things. Then he purposely took me into the side office—and he had a picture of his high school basketball team at Carroll High School. He jokingly said, "By the way, Mike, we used to crush DeMatha. We owned DeMatha."

It was crazy to end up at Notre Dame a year later after I first interviewed. Because when I didn't get it the first time, I looked at Matt and I knew he was only 37 years old. I thought to myself, *Well, there's a young guy at Notre Dame. And I'd love to move to South Bend, but now that'll never be an option in my window.* So I needed to start thinking about other opportunities.

I thought back to a conversation I had with Tubby Raymond, our longtime football coach at Delaware and really an old-school guy. I was the young guy on the coaching staff, and Tubby would come in in August and say, "Mike, I'm gonna keep all these damn fans occupied during the fall. But in December I'm turning them over to you."

I said, "I got you, Coach."

I had been offered the Clemson job after we won the first championship in year three at Delaware. I didn't necessarily want to go, but everybody's reaction seemed to be, "You've got to go. It's an ACC job. You've got to do it because of the money and all that." But I didn't want to go. I liked what we were doing at Delaware.

So I decided I was going to go down the hall to see Tubby because he had turned down jobs. He had been there 40 years, and I was convinced he would talk me out of it. He said, "Come on in, Mike."

I sat down, and he immediately said, "You gotta take it."

I said, "Coach, I look at you, and you've got a great quality of life, you've been here for years."

And he said, "Mike, let me tell you a story. Back in 1967 I was offered the Iowa job. But it was only for $3,000 more, and I knew if I wasn't in the Rose Bowl in three years, they were gonna fire me.

"Mike, I'd be willing to bet that the Clemson job is going to pay a little bit more than $3,000 more than you're making here."

He got me on that one. I walked out of there, and that was not the answer I was looking for. But that was Tubby.

Anyway, it was now the middle of July in South Bend and it was really kind of late to be taking over a new program. I had the players on campus already, and it felt like a really good group. And Torrian Jones, Chris Markwood, and Tom Timmermans were slated to come in as freshmen. They didn't know me; they'd never met me. We were going to fly back to Delaware on the plane the next day—but we grabbed pizza at Bruno's south of town that first night. We took everybody out, and it was really a great chance to meet a lot of people quickly in athletics and at the university.

After we flew back to Delaware, I immediately got in my car and I drove up to watch Torrian, just to meet him. He was up at Pennsbury High School in the Philadelphia area, actually not far from Delaware. I drove up, and his uncles brought him over to a grade-school playground. They were going to work him out, and I'd never seen him play. I was just standing there on the sideline of a playground, and he was playing. I was meeting everybody and I'm telling everybody in sight that everything's going to be great.

Then I drove across the bridge to Philadelphia to meet my point guard, Martin Ingelsby. He had a tough junior year. I got in there, and his mom was really emotional about all this—in a good way. She said, "It's almost like this is a blessing, right? You know this is a blessing because my son will finally have a good year." In my mind there was no option—he had to have a good year. We chatted a little bit longer, and finally I said, "Martin, let's go get some pizza."

So we drove around the corner to a pizza place and we were there for about two hours. I said, "Look, you're my point guard. Tell me what we got."

He told me about all the psyches of everybody on the roster. He ran down their personalities and their games just like he was already a coach. He gave me the whole thing right there. I dropped him back home that night and got back to Delaware really late.

The recruiting period was ongoing, so I was still trying to touch the other guys who were committed. I called Chris Markwood and Tom Timmermans—and I'd met Jones. We also had two more young guys committed. Give Matt credit because he and his staff had done a great job getting those two guys— Jordan Cornette and Chris Thomas. There was no way I wanted to lose Thomas. In fact, I didn't want to lose either one of them, so I went right to Orlando, Florida, to see them play.

They saw me watching them, and I couldn't really talk to parents at that point, but I was bumping into them repeatedly in the restroom. I told them, "Everything will be good."

Then as soon as the dead period ended in August, everybody came up to campus to visit. Chris' father, Frank Thomas, came from Indianapolis to South Bend with his wife, Tammy, and Chris, and we were sitting and talking, and I said, "Look, let's just be honest: one thing has not changed. You know you're going to get the ball as a freshman."

Martin only had the one season left. I said, "I think you can really have fun playing how we're gonna play."

So we kept Chris in the fold. Then Jordan and his parents came up, and Prosser, the Xavier coach, was a great endorser on that one. The Cornettes were from Cincinnati, and Skip was really helpful, telling them they were in good hands at Notre Dame. I really owed him a big thank you for that. When Jordan came to campus, we were visiting and talking, and his family all got to know me. I told him, "Notre Dame's a great fit for you. Nothing's changed."

But he didn't really tell me anything. I was kind of hanging now, waiting for him to tell me he was going to stay on board. The Cornettes all left, and I was walking out of the old offices. Then Jordan came sprinting around the corner in the hallway and he said, "Coach, Coach, I want you to know I'm coming to Notre Dame. I guess I forgot to say that." We still laugh about that.

You know who else really helped me with the current players and all the parents? John MacLeod. He was absolutely fabulous. Matt Carroll's dad called me and said, "Coach, we've done our homework. We've talked to Coach MacLeod, and he said we're in great hands with you."

I said, "Well, I appreciate Coach saying that. I'm really excited to work with your son."

So Coach MacLeod, whom I called in August, was really good to us, especially with the current players and parents. He told them not to worry. I think what he was saying was that it was a maybe a little tumultuous with Matt leaving after just a year, and he wanted the players he'd recruited to know they were going to be in a good situation. That was his theme.

So it all worked out great. We kept Chris Thomas and Jordan Cornette, who Matt and his staff had done a great job getting here. We also had Ryan Humphrey, who had transferred from Oklahoma and had to sit out a year; he was warming up in the bullpen. So when you look back at all the circumstances, John and Matt had set this thing up nicely for us.

I have a funny story about having a Cornette and a Cornett on the roster. After I came home off the road that very first summer, Skip Meyer, our basketball trainer, came into my office and said the parents of one of our recruits were down in the Center at volleyball camp. Meyer said it was the Cornett family. Now I know we've got Jordan Cornette committed. But Meyer said this kid was a junior, and I'm thinking, *But I know Jordan Cornette is a senior.*

So I went down and I sat with the parents. I was with big Rick and his wife, and their daughter was playing in our Notre Dame volleyball camp. Now I was really flying blind here. Skip didn't understand that I was still a little lost, and I was trying hard to be cordial. This was July, and it was a month before I met Jordan and his group in August. I said, "Your son looking forward to a big senior year?"

And they said, "Well, he's only going to be a junior."

I thought, *Well, I'm pretty sure Jordan Cornette is a rising senior.*

So now I'm so confused that I'm just trying to massage it and fake it and get through it. I said, "Hey, we'll get you up for a football game, for an official visit."

And they said, "Coach, he can't make an official visit because he's only a junior."

By now I'm wondering what in the world is going on. We got back together as a staff, and I said, "I thought Jordan Cornette was a senior; I just met his parents down on the court at volleyball camp."

And now they all figured it out. "No, that's Rick Cornett, he's a junior." So I said, "Oh, we've got two—a Cornett and a Cornette. I got it!" So those were the things that happen when you're just learning who is who.

My staff came together, too. Sean Kearney was in the air as I was interviewing at Notre Dame. He was going to Las Vegas for the last weekend of the recruiting period and recruiting for Delaware. I told him, "I'll let you know what happens." He landed, and I had left him a voicemail. I said, "We're heading to South Bend. I'll call you tomorrow."

All he had was his Delaware gear, so he went to Dick's Sporting Goods and bought Notre Dame T-shirts. He said, "I'll never forget it. I was in the Hertz line listening to my voicemail messages. I'm thinking, *Damn, this is pretty good.*"

Then we hired Lewis Preston from Coastal Carolina. He had worked there for Pete Strickland, who was a good friend of mine. Rod Balanis came in the beginning as the ops guy, and I had known Rod forever. I knew Anthony Solomon from the ACC days, back to when he was a player at Virginia and I thought he'd be great as a coach. And Sean was my right-hand man, and I felt good about that.

After I got the job in the middle of the summer, our family lived in a house on Angela Boulevard on a temporary basis from August until December. Our whole staff moved into our permanent houses in December, and it was the worst snowstorm ever, which represented the tumult of getting situated for that first season.

The Early Years

2000–01 (20–10, 11–5 Big East)

NCAA Midwest Regional: W 83–71 vs. Xavier, L 68–56 vs. Ole Miss

Big East West Division champion

Big East Tournament: L 66–54 vs. Pittsburgh (quarterfinal)

Starters:

- G   Martin Ingelsby (captain), Sr., 6'0", 8.2 points
- G   Matt Carroll, So., 6'6", 12.4 points
- F   Troy Murphy (captain), Jr., 6'11", 21.8 points, first-team NCAA consensus All-American, Big East Player of the Year
- F   Ryan Humphrey, Jr., 6'8", 14.1 points
- F   David Graves, Jr., 6'6", 13.8 points
- F   Harold Swanagan, Jr., 6'7", 4.2 points

THAT FIRST YEAR AT NOTRE DAME CAME SO QUICKLY, BUT I FELT comfortable because I'd lived on the East Coast and I kind of knew the Big East Conference. I'd watched lots of Big East basketball and I understood the university's mission, academics, and culture. I knew what I was getting into. I knew what we could do in terms of recruiting. I kind of had a feel for all that.

When practice started I was very conscious that we were going to make it work with six guys—Troy Murphy, David

Graves, Martin Ingelsby, Ryan Humphrey, Matt Carroll, and Harold Swanagan. I put our starters—actually those six guys—in the gold jerseys, and it stayed that way. I never put anybody else in gold for a month. It probably hurt the development of guys like Torrian Jones or Tom Timmermans, but my feeling was that these six guys would run things and set the tone. My biggest worry was the conversation I was going to have with Swanagan because he had started, but now Hump was eligible and he was going to play.

I just gave Ingelsby the ball. He was the senior. I needed him to be the quarterback. I was so very lucky that I inherited a senior point guard like that the first year. Certainly we had Hump and Murph, two really big-time players, but when you've got a senior point guard, he's going to play the whole game and he won't make mistakes. Carroll was a rock solid guy; he was growing up. So it was a neat group.

I had done my homework. I knew coming in that Hump had been sitting out a year. I knew Chris Thomas was committed, that Matt Doherty had done a great job there. After I got hired, I remember other basketball people telling me, "You know you've got a heck of a team there—Troy Murphy, the Big East Player of the Year. You've got this guy, Ryan Humphrey, eligible to play." I'm thinking, *Geez, this is an even better job than I thought.*

But we had to get in the NCAA Tournament that first year. That same group had just missed the year before, and I knew we had to get in for everybody's credibility, including mine, moving forward.

With Murph it was all about moving him around on the court. In our style there was a freedom for him to play and certainly there was an understanding that he needed to get touches. And Hump's presence let Murph be Murph. Hump knew his year was coming and he really let Murph do his thing. That was one thing I was worried about.

There was a little bit of tension at times with Murph and me. Coming out of a timeout against Syracuse at home where we won, he was intent on playing in the center of the Syracuse zone. I never argued with him. I said, "I like that idea." He did it, it worked, and it turned out to be one of those great things.

We beat a bunch of good teams that first year. We beat a Syracuse team ranked No. 8 in the poll and won at Georgetown and Boston College when they were both top 10 teams. The one I remember most was against Cincinnati. That game was early, but they were ranked No. 16, and that was our first bit of credibility. We put it on them pretty good down there. I basically was having an anxiety attack the night before the game. I knew this would be a chance for us to do something and I think I slept one hour. That bus ride home was the most pleasant ever because I felt a little bit more accepted. We had won a big game against a ranked team, and I think our group kind of felt, *Man, we're pretty good.*

The crossroads of that first season came when we played at Kentucky in the middle of January. We went to Lexington, and the Wildcats kicked our butts by 11, and maybe it wasn't that close. I came into the locker room and I hadn't really gotten on anybody yet that year. I didn't know them well enough. I challenged them, asked them if they were tough enough. My language was probably a little salty, and I was a little nervous because there's a priest in the locker room. Father Bill Seetch was there with us. As I was going into the coaches' locker room, Swan—who was from Kentucky, as was David Graves—got up and threw a Gatorade canister and backed up everything I had just said. He said, "He's right. Screw this. This is my home state. We came down here and played like babies."

I walked in the coaches' locker room and I looked at Father Bill and I said, "Okay, Father, what do I do now?" And Father Bill said, "You're right, Coach. You were right. Great job." So I thought, *I guess it's okay to get after them a little bit—even at Notre Dame.*"

My son, Kyle, was on that Kentucky trip as an 11-year-old little kid and he absolutely remembers that scene. He said to me, "You were honest with them, and then Swan gets after it when you're done." I said to assistant coach Rod Balanis, "Maybe we've got a chance. Maybe they believe me."

We were 9–5 at that point and then we won eight in a row after that in the Big East. I had seriously wondered as we came back from Lexington if we could get a bid. What a waste of talent of that group it would've been if we couldn't get to the NCAA Tournament. I was really hard on myself. More than a few times I thought, *I can't believe you can't get these guys to the tournament. This is an NCAA Tournament team.*

In early February we were on a good run, playing Pittsburgh at Fitzgerald Fieldhouse. We had won four Big East games in a row—including against those very good Syracuse and Georgetown teams in the last two. And Pitt was good, so the law of averages said we were probably due to take a loss.

We had a meeting the night before the game. I said, "Fellas, I want to be honest with you. I've been around this game a long time. We've won four in a row in this league. You know most teams now playing Pittsburgh here, they just take the L. Life's been good, and everybody is telling us how good we are. But if you get this one tomorrow, you're showing signs of being a special team." Their eyes brightened. They grasped that. We played great and won on the road there. That's when they kind of said, "Let's win the West. We can win the West."

We were in Blacksburg, Virginia, to play Virginia Tech on a Saturday night, and then the regular season was going to end on Big Monday at UConn in one of our last regular-season games. Remember that I was a little younger then, and maybe I was feeling it a little bit. We were warming up in Blacksburg, and the result of the Syracuse-Georgetown game had a bearing on whether we won the West Division in the league. If Georgetown beat Syracuse, we could win the West. Our guys were walking out for the opening tip, they were still about 30 seconds from starting, and assistant coach Sean Kearney grabbed me and said, "Georgetown got 'em."

I said to our guys, "Come on back for a minute." I told them, "This is for the West Division title, and if we win, we're gonna put a banner up and we get rings." And our guys' eyes were like saucers because that was new territory for Notre Dame back then.

We played great and we won by 24. I told associate head coach Rod Balanis with about three minutes to go—when we were up about 15—to go in the locker room and draw a banner on the board. So when we got in there, we had a banner. It was foreign territory, but it was very exciting to talk about that, to be able to use all that as a motivation. That group really responded to it.

We took our charter that Sunday to Springfield, Massachusetts, and stopped at the Naismith Basketball Hall of Fame, which served as a neat way to educate our team on basketball history. UConn was having a bit of a down year. I was still feeling it a little bit after we had won Saturday and so I asked a UConn reporter, "Do you think that if they beat us, they'll storm the court?" I actually said that. Someone told me later that Jim Calhoun's reaction was, "What are you talking about? We're three years removed from winning a national championship. We don't storm the court for anyone."

So that wasn't a really good thing for a rookie head coach to say before a game. Before the game started, I made a point to go talk to Calhoun, and I said, "Coach, I was completely out of line. I was feeling my oats a little bit there." And he just looked at me. They beat our butts that night 75–59, but it didn't matter in the standings because we had won the West Division. And despite that awkward start, Jim and I grew to have a great relationship.

We had a good seed in the Big East Tournament because we won the division, but we ended up losing to Pittsburgh in the first round. We were locked for an NCAA bid because we had 11 league wins. But I said something, probably being a little young, along the lines of, "I don't know if we can invest in both tournaments, so which one do you want?" Some people thought I didn't care enough about the Big East Tournament. That comment wasn't accepted really well. Now people say we invest too much in the ACC Tournament and we're too tired for the NCAA.

But it was just awesome to get back in the NCAA Tournament in 2001. It was neat for that team, but it didn't really hit me until Selection Sunday how it was Notre Dame's first appearance in such a long time. When I took the job, I would have said, "Well, Notre Dame hasn't been in it for three or four years." But 10 years? I never would have thought that. You felt like all of our basketball people were thinking, *Finally, we're back.*

We went to Kansas City, Missouri, for the first weekend of the NCAA Tournament. Kearney and I looked at each other as we were standing in the tunnel after our team had taken the floor at Kemper Arena. It was Notre Dame's first NCAA Tournament appearance in a decade, and the Victory March was echoing up the tunnel. We kind of looked at each other, and I said, "Okay, this is pretty good. This is really cool."

We played really well against Xavier, winning 83–71 in the first round. Then we had a chance against a really good Ole Miss team in the second round but just couldn't finish it and lost by three. But we felt good about the first year and we felt good about getting back to the NCAA Tournament. It gave me and our program some great initial credibility.

But I give a lot of credit to John MacLeod and Doherty because they left me and our staff with really good players to coach. The starting front line my first year included two first-round NBA picks—Murph and Hump. Carroll started on the wing and he ended up playing five years in the NBA. So you just had some real men who were ripe to win, and they really did a great job taking ownership of themselves.

Always in my mind, I was thinking what these guys as players already had been through. They'd played for MacLeod and Doherty—two completely different personalities with completely different approaches. So from my end, there was a lot of just trying to manage this situation as best I could. I hoped they would just take it upon themselves to go out there and say, "Hey, we've got to get to the NCAA Tournament," which they did.

When we got to March, I thought back on one particular comment I had made in that very first meeting in the locker room: "You want to go to the NCAA Tournament? I think I can help you with that with my experience."

Carroll, Ingelsby, and Swan—those guys were my rocks. I'm always thankful to that whole group that they allowed me to coach them. Given what they'd been through, I had to earn that. But we had great memories, and even though his time here was really complicated, Murph has really come around to Notre Dame again and he appreciates the place.

That first year I needed an endorsement of a veteran guy because I wasn't sure they were buying my stuff. For example, Murph had a lot on the line. So there was a little heat on me. I was so relieved at the end of that year when Murph had his big year, became the Big East Player of the Year, and we got to the NCAA Tournament. We got on the plane after that loss to Mississippi in the second round of the NCAA Tournament, and I thought, *Whew. We got back to the NCAA Tournament and Murph's going to be a lottery pick. I didn't screw this thing up.*

When Murph put his name in to go to the NBA, there was a lot of reaction. Some of it was negative—even from our own people. I disagreed with anyone who wanted to take issue with that. This guy played for three head coaches in three years, led us back to the NCAA Tournament, and was going to be a lottery pick. We needed to lead the parade out of town.

I got a call from Gene DeFilippo, who was athletic director at Boston College back then. He said, "I love how you handled that with Murph."

You don't play head games with this kid and try to tell him he needs to come back because it's Notre Dame and he needs to be a four-year guy. That was the right time for him. Those were some interesting dynamics, but it was the right decision given all the different circumstances.

2001–02 (22–11, 10–6 Big East)

NCAA South Regional: W 82–63 vs. UNC-Charlotte, L 84–77 vs. Duke

Big East Tournament: W 83–63 vs. St. John's (quarterfinal), L 82–77 vs. Connecticut (semifinal)

Starters:

G   Chris Thomas, Fr., 6'1", 15.6 points, National Freshman of the Year, Big East Rookie of the Year

G   Matt Carroll, Jr., 6'6", 14.1 points

G   David Graves (captain), Sr., 6'6", 14.4 points

F   Ryan Humphrey (captain), Sr., 6'8", 18.9 points, second-team All-American, first-team All-Big East

F   Harold Swanagan (captain), Sr., 6'7", 8.1 points

I had a great team, a good group coming back the second year with Matt Carroll, David Graves, and Chris Thomas in the mix. We handed Chris the ball, and we had Harold Swanagan and Ryan Humphrey inside. We were old again; it was the get-old, stay-old thing. Torrian Jones and Jordan Cornette both came off the bench little bit, and Tom Timmermans gave us some good minutes. Troy Murphy and Martin Ingelsby were gone, and yet we really got out of the gate strong. We competed really well in Hawaii and started 7–0.

Thomas got a triple-double in his first college game. He burst on the scene, and it was everything he was advertised to be. We were playing well, and Humphrey and Swanagan were just men up front. David Graves and Carroll were physical and tough, and we had the young, free-wheeling guard to run stuff. We swept Pitt when the Panthers had a top 10 RPI and we went four overtimes to win at Georgetown. Those were the power wins that kept us a strong contender for the NCAA Tournament.

We won at Miami late when the Hurricanes were ranked No. 17. Carroll was hurt, and Jones played 29 minutes and played fabulously. Thomas had 32 points and a dozen assists. We scored 51 points in the second half of that game on the road. That was our 10th league win, and that pretty much got us a bid into the NCAA Tournament again.

The Georgetown game was crazy. It went four overtimes. We just keep playing. Guys were fouling out all over the place. I tried to put Timmermans back in during the third overtime. Assistant Sean Kearney finally had to tell me, "He's already fouled out." I remember turning to Kearney and going, "Well, who is eligible? Who can we put in the game?" We ran a set that we call two-cross, and Carroll hit a big three. He finished with 30.

The Hoyas had the ball with a shot to win it three times— at the end of regulation and two of the overtimes. We dodged a couple of bullets and ended up escaping. Graves came off the bench and played 49 minutes—that was crazy. Michael Sweetney had 35 points and 22 rebounds against us. Thomas played the whole way, going all 60 minutes. At 116–111, it was the highest-scoring game in Big East history. And until our five-overtime game with Louisville, it was the longest game in league history.

It was the talk of college basketball, and that win really kind of gave us confidence. We still have footage of Hump coming out with about seven seconds left and the game in hand. He came over to me, we're both smiling, and he gave me a big hug on the sideline. I'll never forget that visual. We were both laughing and thinking, *Can you believe this?* That's a great memory.

We beat the heck out of UNC-Charlotte in the first NCAA game there in Greenville, South Carolina. Danny White was our walk-on that year. Now the athletics director at Central Florida, he was the son of our then-athletic director Kevin White. We were up so big that Danny played four minutes in an NCAA Tournament game. I remember grabbing him in the hallway in front of his dad, and I said, "You just played four minutes of an NCAA Tournament game. You owe me!" And we all just laughed. Danny dealt with a bunch of injuries, but that was a great experience for him.

Then there was so much attention on the second-round game against Duke because of the connections. Now I was facing my mentor, and he always beat his assistants. I don't feel the NCAA did this intentionally; the bracket just kind of fell that way. But it was a little distracting to me. Mike Krzyzewski was so great before the game. He was awesome. But it was such a dagger because we had that one won. We had Chris on the line. We were up six with about four or five minutes to go. He had shot 90 percent from the line. He missed the one-and-one, and Daniel Ewing immediately hit a three at the other end.

Hump basically played his way into the first round of the NBA draft that day with 15 points and 12 rebounds against Carlos Boozer. It was so disappointing because we were right there. But that was a fun team for me because they really allowed me to coach them. Now I was in.

Hump was the last player off the bus every road game. And he'd reach over and just grab my shoulder while walking off the bus. When your main guy gives you a little squeeze as if, "We're going to be all right, Coach," that makes you feel better. He always did that as a senior. That group allowed me to coach more. You could help them more—and they were more accepting. That was a fun year with great, great leadership.

2002–03 (24–10, 10–6 Big East)

NCAA West Regional: W 70–69 vs. UW-Milwaukee, W 68–60 vs. Illinois, L 88–71 vs. Arizona

Big East Tournament: L 83–80 vs. St. John's (first round)

Starters:

- G   Chris Thomas, So., 6'1", 18.7 points
- G   Matt Carroll (captain), Sr., 6'6", 19.5 points, first-team All-Big East
- F   Jordan Cornette, So., 6'9", 3.0 points
- F   Dan Miller (captain), Sr., 6'8", 13.9 points
- F   Torin Francis, Fr., 6'11", 11.1 points

We had lost Ryan Humphrey, Harold Swanagan, and David Graves, who were real men. Instead of going to freshmen, we went to Dan Miller, a real veteran who was a McDonald's All American. And after transferring to Notre Dame from Maryland, he had a chip on his shoulder.

We played Maryland that year in the BB&T Classic in D.C. And Miller had a great edge to his game; he could be a brutal competitor. I talked to him before the Maryland game because I didn't want him to be distracted, but before I got anywhere, he said, "Don't worry, Coach. I'm fine." He hit a three one time and ran right in front of the Maryland bench. He was ready that night.

We won that one against a Maryland team that was ranked ninth and then we beat a Texas team that was ranked second. Chris Thomas, Torin Francis, and Miller played great. That was three top 10 victories in a week with the win earlier that week against Marquette and Dwyane Wade.

That put us on the scene. Miller was the ultimate mercenary to keep us old and keep that edge. Thomas was still playing like a son of a gun, and Matty Carroll was one of the better guards around.

Jordan Cornette came off the bench with Tom Timmermans, and they gave us good role stuff and provided good defense.

During the recruitment of Miller, I said, "We want him," but assistant Sean Kearney asked, "Well, why would we want a guy here for just a year?"

I said, "That's a great point." Nobody was doing the one-year transfer thing back then, which has become so common now. But I thought one year could be a big difference-maker. I coached his brother Greg at Delaware and knew the family very well.

And Dan Miller was a key to get us back in the NCAA Tournament the third year in 2002–03. We dodged Bruce Pearl's UW-Milwaukee team in the first round in Indianapolis. At the very end of the game, Milwaukee's Clay Tucker drove and passed to Dylan Page, whose layup rolled off the front rim. Thomas still says he got a hand on that shot at the end; I'm not sure about that. Then Miller flat shot us to the Sweet 16. He was bombing away in the second-round game against Illinois. It was Bill Self's last game at Illinois. They had Deron Williams, a terrific guard who went on to become an NBA All-Star. The Illini were young and they were gifted, and we just shot the heck out of the ball. As a team we made 13 threes, and Miller had five of them.

It was a great ride from Indy back to South Bend because we were going to the Sweet 16. But Miller set the tone while firing from deep. Until we went to the Elite Eight, Miller for a long time always joked, "Remember, I got you to the second weekend; nobody else has done that."

It was a heck of a group. We dealt with Thomas testing the NBA waters that spring. He worked out for about 20 teams and at the end of the day he decided to come back.

2003–04 (19–13, 9–7 Big East)

NIT: W 71–59 vs. Purdue, W 77–66 vs. St. Louis, L 65–61 vs.
Oregon

Big East Tournament: W 65–64 vs. West Virginia (first round), L
66–58 vs. Connecticut (quarterfinal)

Starters:

- G Chris Thomas (captain), Jr., 6'1", 19.7 points
- G Chris Quinn, So., 6'2", 14.3 points
- G Torrian Jones, Sr., 6'4", 8.4 points
- F Jordan Cornette (captain), Jr., 6'9", 5.8 points
- F Torin Francis (captain); So., 6'11", 14.2 points
- C Tom Timmermans (captain), Sr.; 6'11", 6.0 points

2004–05 (17–12, 9–7 Big East)

NIT: L 78–73 vs. Holy Cross

Big East Tournament: L 72–65 vs. Rutgers (first round)

Starters:

- G Chris Thomas (captain), Sr., 6'1", 14.2 points
- G Chris Quinn (captain), Jr., 6–2, 12.6 points
- G Colin Falls, So., 6'4", 12.6 points.
- F Jordan Cornette (captain), Sr., 6'9", 4.2 points
- F Torin Francis (captain), Jr., 6'11", 9.3 points

2005–06 (16–14, 6–10 Big East)

NIT: W 79–69 vs. Vanderbilt, L 87–84 vs. Michigan (2OT)

Big East Tournament: L 67–63 vs. Georgetown (first round)

Starters:

- G Russell Carter, Jr., 6'4", 11.5 points
- G Chris Quinn (captain), Sr., 6'2", 17.7 points, first-team All-
Big East
- G Colin Falls, Jr., 6'4", 13.8 points
- F Rob Kurz, So., 6'9", 6.4 points
- F Torin Francis (captain), Sr., 6'11", 11.6 points

We went to the NIT three years in a row. The first year Chris Quinn got hurt in the Big East Tournament. At 9–7 in the league, we were right on the edge. That year was the first time the Big East went to the mini-conference in terms of scheduling. And it was Notre Dame, Pittsburgh, Connecticut, and Syracuse who played each other twice. Mike Tranghese, the Big East Conference commissioner, did that to provide more television coverage, and I always used to say, "Well, we're playing the A schedule again."

I'm not sure the NCAA Selection Committee understood the unbalanced schedule because I think we were the first league to do it. We went 9–7 two of those years, and our strength of schedule in the league was way different than a lot of people realized. But I don't know how much they weighed that.

I always thought one of those years we should have gotten in. We lost to Oregon at home in the NIT in 2004, and the next year we got beat by Holy Cross in the first round. So I came to Notre Dame, got the program back to the NCAA Tournament, and then to a Sweet 16. You think you're untouchable, but then we go to three NITs, and the natives were a little restless. People were saying, "Can we ever get back? We don't do this; we don't do that."

Year Seven became so pivotal because it was swinging against you a little bit. Yet Kevin White, our athletic director, was amazingly supportive and understood the big picture. I was a young head coach still—and I was trying to prove myself and be secure and confident.

2006–07 (24–8, 11–5 Big East)

NCAA Midwest Regional: L 74–64 vs. Winthrop

Big East Tournament: W 89–83 vs. Syracuse (quarterfinal), L 84-82
   vs. Georgetown (semifinal)

Starters:

   G   Russell Carter (captain), Sr., 6'4", 17.1 points, first-team
       All-Big East

   G   Tory Jackson, Fr., 5'11", 8.0 points

   G   Colin Falls (captain), Sr., 6'5", 15.3 points, first-team All-
       Big East

   F   Rob Kurz (captain), Jr., 6'9", 12.6 points

   F   Luke Harangody, Fr., 6'8", 11.6 points

Year Seven was a real key. I walked in on Media Day
in October that year and said, "We've got to get back to the
NCAA Tournament." That's what we had to do. It wasn't any
more complicated than that. Then we lost Kyle McAlarney to
the suspension. As just a freshman, Tory Jackson stepped in and
ran our team. Luke Harangody developed into an unbelievable
weapon as a freshman; he kind of came out of nowhere. We had
the seniors, Colin Falls and Russ Carter, doing a really good
job. Rob Kurz was solid, and I was just relieved to get back in
the dance.

McAlarney was out of school for the spring semester after
he was caught with marijuana in his car. I thought to myself,
Oh, boy, thank God for Tory Jackson. In fact, thank God for both
Harangody and Jackson. They had to play big roles, maybe bigger
than we thought, for us to scratch out a bid. Jackson had to take
over once the conference schedule started. We beat Louisville
here at home in our first league game, which I thought gave him,
our team, and the coaches great confidence. Harangody became a

starter and he was just scoring for us and doing all kinds of stuff. And we got back into the NCAA Tournament.

Now, in the midst of all that, we had to save McAlarney. We didn't want him leaving on a bad note. But he didn't want to come back. He was embarrassed. His parents were mad; everybody was mad. McAlarney had been suspended, but he was going to get his final decision from the administration on a Friday afternoon in late January. We were scheduled to fly to New York that same day in advance of Saturday's St. John's game. I told Kyle I would pick him up at the main building. We had practiced from 3:00 to 4:30 PM, and the team was already on the bus. I told them, "I'll meet you guys at the airport."

Kyle came walking out, and it was bad news. So I drove around with him a little bit. It was really hard because I went to the back of the plane to tell our guys it was official he was gone— and I broke up.

I told Martin Ingelsby, who was our operations guy at the time, "You're staying here, go find him. I don't want him alone tonight." But Martin couldn't find him. We were still waiting on the plane, and probably 45 minutes later, Ingelsby finally came back. It turned out McAlarney just got in his car and drove to an uncle's house in Cincinnati and then eventually drove the rest of the way home to New York.

We played Providence at home on a Thursday in mid-February, and so I gave Kyle a call. His AAU guy, Tony Sagona, already was getting calls. The word was out that McAlarney was going to go visit Xavier in a day or so. Michigan State was on him and so was Florida. We were sitting in the basketball offices on a Sunday in a staff meeting and we were talking about Kyle. I said, "I can't get him to pick up the phone."

And I give Pat Holmes, our academic adviser, a lot of credit because I was thinking about a lot of different things, including how our team would react. We had Providence coming in and we needed a win to keep our NCAA Tournament hopes alive. And Pat said, "Anybody thought about getting on a plane out there?"

I said, "That's a great idea."

So I left the next day. I finally got him on the phone and I said, "Kyle, I would like to come to your house Monday night." I let the assistants run practice.

I told Ingelsby to get me Kyle's black jersey. So I had it in my bag. I went to the McAlarneys' house. From what I could tell, they had a lot of nails on the wall because they had had Notre Dame stuff up there, which had been taken down. I walked in, and his mother, Janice, crushed me for 45 minutes. And I understood. She was just being a mom and she was letting it fly. Kyle just sat there quietly.

After about an hour, Kyle's dad kind of tried to bring it back to the middle a little bit. It looked like I had one ally.

My whole selling point was this: "We could have had better communication. But the university rule is the rule. It's pretty clear cut; it's in our handbook. I know you've got a lot of people that want you, but Kyle, here's the thing: you have to sit out there. You're eligible at Notre Dame right away. You can come back in the summer and get your credits. Kyle, give me a little credit, too. Our system is pretty good for you. You're in the midst of a great career. So think about that. Think about the eligibility."

I knew he loved his teammates—Ryan Ayers, Zach Hillesland, Jackson. "Come on, think about your teammates, man. These are your guys," I said. And so we got through it. I said, "Look, I've got a car waiting outside." And I knew it was a good sign because Kyle wanted to drive me back to the airport hotel. I said, "Nope,

I'm good." I was staying at the Marriott at the Newark airport and I had the first flight back Tuesday to get ready for Providence. I said, "I gotta go. I have to get our group ready for Providence. But I just think it's your destiny. You made a mistake, but people will understand."

Then I threw him the jersey. As I left I said, "Hey, you may want to try this on."

I walked out the door. And he teared up a little bit when he caught it.

I thought, *Okay, there's at least a chance.*

We were in a staff meeting Tuesday afternoon before practice, and the staff was asking me what I thought. And right then Kyle called, and I said, "We're going to find out right here."

Kyle said, "Coach, you're right. I need to come back. I need to finish there."

I said, "Kyle, I'm thrilled. I think it's the right decision. You're a Notre Dame man. You should have a degree from here. You should finish with these other guys you came in with. Right now, though, I've got to get to practice and help your brothers get ready."

He said, "Coach, go get them ready."

I said, "I'll call you tomorrow."

So that was a great story for our program that he came back and finished. And obviously he's so proud to be a Notre Dame guy. He's going to retire from playing and take his high school coaching job next year. He's coming back to Staten Island, New York, and going to be the coach and athletic director at Bishop Moore Catholic High School.

People talk about the great memories at Notre Dame. And I know we've had some great wins. But that's maybe one of the best memories because that was all about being a teacher. That was being an educator. At the end of the year, we got the NCAA bid. We got knocked out by Winthrop in Spokane, Washington. But we got there. Given the loss of Kyle, we had almost maxed out who we were to get the bid. There wasn't a lot left in the tank emotionally.

We brought our two freshmen, Harangody and Jackson, to the NCAA press conference after that game. We were waiting to go up, and I was so excited, even though we lost, and talking to them about the next year. They had been so instrumental and they were only going to be sophomores. I said, "Fellas, we're going to do this and we're going to do that."

And I think they thought I was nuts. They were looking at me, "Coach, we just lost."

But that was one where I turned the page quick. I think psychologically I just wanted to get through that year. I needed to talk about something else.

We were at the crossroads a little bit going into that season. I actually thought to myself, *If we go to a fourth NIT, I don't know if I want to deal with that.*

Jobs had opened after the previous season, and I called Mike Krzyzewski, and Mike K was great. He said, "You stay the course; you're a Notre Dame guy. I want you to do something. What's the weather up there?" Because he always gives me a hard time about our weather.

I said, "Coach, it's a pretty nice day here in April."

He said, "I want you to walk around campus for an hour. Just walk around campus, just appreciate what you've got."

So I did. I walked around and I came back. He was right, of course. I stayed the course and thank God I did. We got the bid, we got back in, and then we went to the NCAA Tournament nine out of the next 11 years.

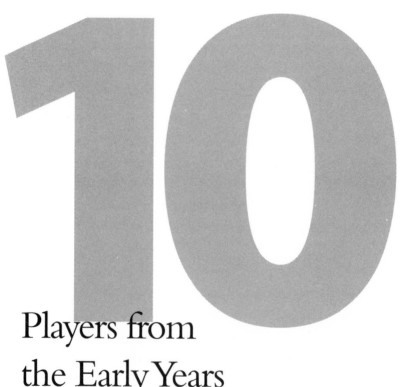

10

Players from the Early Years

TROY MURPHY

When I got to Notre Dame, my biggest worry was that I was Troy Murphy's third coach in three years. So would he let me coach him? I knew it was going to take a while to earn his respect. I came in knowing I had an unbelievable sales job to do to get him to buy in that I could help him. And it took me about half a season for me to really reach him. I went into it thinking on a daily basis, *How do I go at him today?*

Fortunately, I was able to communicate through Martin Ingelsby, Matt Carroll, and Harold Swanagan to kind of get the rest of the group to buy in. But I thought by midseason or by the end of January, Murph was kind of a believer. He was enjoying winning—and we were winning. He was able to say, "Gosh, we're going to go to the NCAA Tournament. I've never played in it." And Notre Dame hadn't been in it for awhile.

Luckily, Tony Sagona, his AAU coach, who was his guy, was selling me and so were some of the other people around him. Murph could be a stubborn one, which is why he was great, but he also had a great sense of humor and he was a guy that I used to kid around with a lot. He lived on the first floor of Morrissey Hall as a junior, but he never used the door. He kept the window popped and would crawl in and out of his window. He was famous for being a late-night workout guy. He'd come back to the Joyce Center and shoot until midnight, and then I'd hear from the security guys on campus, "We saw Murph climbing in his window last night." That's just how he rolled.

RYAN HUMPHREY

I did my homework when I came to Notre Dame. Ryan Humphrey came here because Matt Doherty told him he could be a three man and not a four man anymore. He liked that idea of facing the bucket. When I got here, I said, "Let's do lunch." And one of the great first meetings we had was when I met him on campus in North Dining Hall. I knew he was concerned, too, because he'd transferred with a certain thing in mind and he had a chance to be a pro. So that's another psyche I had to really learn. I needed to earn his trust—just like with Troy Murphy. With those two guys, I had a lot of work to do.

We got the salt and pepper shakers out and did Xs and Os on the table. I said, "I know you really want to face the bucket. I get it and I'll get you there." But I said, "I want to get us in some high-low stuff with you and Murph." So I had the pepper guy up high, and Murph was the salt down low. I said, "You're the pepper," and he laughed. I was trying to loosen him up. I told him, "I'll get you facing from there, driving from there, shooting your 15-foot jump shot. But I don't know about just putting you outside the arc. I don't know if that's best for you and us and our future. But you gotta trust me. I'll get you facing the bucket."

So he was good. He needed that special touch, and we needed him. We were three around two with high-low action, and those two guys pounded people in high-low situations. And he shot some 15-foot jump shots, and he drove it from there.

A year later we were going into Hump's senior year. Rod Balanis was our ops guy and he came running in my office. Keep in mind it was July. He said, "Coach, Coach, I just walked through the Pit. Hump's shooting three-point shots. We're in trouble."

I said, "Don't say a word. I can only keep a guy in his role about four months. Darned if I'm going to try and do anything in July." Rod was still excited, and I said, "We'll revisit that."

And of course, in Hump's senior year, we played big sometimes. It was great because if Hump missed a jump shot early, I didn't have to say a word. He'd go inside; he'd get back down there. His senior year he knew how he was playing and how we had it set up for him. He was going to be a draft pick and he ended up making himself into a first-round pick in great part because of the way he played in the NCAA Tournament. He ended up as the 19th overall pick of the Orlando Magic. So we were really pleased that it worked out. Hump's line to me now is, "You got me paid twice" because we hired him here at Notre Dame as an assistant coach.

DAVID GRAVES

David Graves had a really high basketball IQ. He may have made as many clutch shots as anybody in our history. He wanted to be coached, and I think we developed a really strong relationship. It was tested a little bit because when we got on our run at the end of my first year, we were bringing him off the bench. He struggled with that at times, but he did come off the bench during that period, gave us production, and was still playing starter's minutes.

The night before the Virginia Tech game late in my first season, he came to my room in the hotel and he was not real pleased. But he played great the next day and we won the Big East West Division. Then we decided to start him for the NCAA

Tournament, and he went 7-for-7 from the field in the first round against a Xavier team led by David West and just played great.

In the beginning with Ryan Humphrey and Troy Murphy, there was a little bit of uncertainty and they weren't quite ready to trust me yet. But David was more like, "I'm glad you're here, Coach. Coach me." He didn't like coming off the bench during that one period, but he knew it was for the best. And then when we started him, he delivered.

HAROLD SWANAGAN

Harold Swanagan was the ultimate rock and a real believer right away. I was very lucky to have him. One of my biggest worries that first year was that Ryan Humphrey was now eligible and deserved to start, even though Swan had been the starter. I probably lost sleep for a couple of nights trying to figure out how to approach Swan about starting Hump.

I grabbed him outside the training room because I didn't want to make it some big meeting. Our first exhibition game was maybe three days away. I said, "Hey, Swan, I just want to talk to you." I'd been mixing the jerseys up in practice, so nobody could really tell exactly what the lineup would be. Those six guys were all playing. I said, "I'm going to start Hump with Troy inside on Friday."

And he cut me off and said, "Coach, whatever you need me to do, man, I'm there." I hadn't earned that with him yet, and that's why he's always been very special to me. I'm thrilled that he's back with me now. He was always very special because that could have been a problem, and it wasn't. He just took the high road, came off the bench, and started again for a while later in the year. He was always a believer in what's best for the team. He's been awesome.

Martin Ingelsby

Martin Ingelsby was my steadying force. I got the head coaching job at Notre Dame and I immediately had this four-year guy who had a chip on his shoulder because he didn't play much the year before. He hadn't been starting, but he was a senior. He turned out to be a rock because of his basketball IQ. You knew back then he was going to be a coach because you could just really communicate with him.

When I was at Duke, we came up to Philly to recruit Rafal Bigus, a Polish kid who eventually went to Villanova. So Mike Krzyzewski, Tommy Amaker, and I went up and watched an open gym at Carroll High School. Tom Ingelsby was the coach, and Martin was a ninth-grader. We were commenting even then, "He's going to be a heck of a guard." And I remembered him. I was in the Delaware area so had heard a lot about him.

In my first meeting with him, I said, "Tell me about our team. I trust you completely. Who do you like?" He gave me the rundown on skillset, attitude, personality, concerns.

My son, Kyle, had a great line. He said, "Dad, I just don't like when you take Martin out because everything's under control when he's in."

And I said, "Kyle, you're 14, but you're exactly right."

Martin was always my daughter Callie's guy, too. She loved him. He went with her to show and tell one day at her school. That's the kind of guy he was. So you know he had the assistant's job after that.

Matt Carroll

John MacLeod was really helpful with the Carroll family. Coach was very close with them, and Matt Carroll's father called him and said, "What about Mike Brey?" Coach endorsed me so I'll always be thankful to him for that. Matt Carroll was a believer right away—like David Graves and Martin Ingelsby. And he was unbelievably gifted. I was able to assure him: "No one's going to mess with your role. I know how you play. You're a shooter, and we're going to get you shots. Here's how we're going to play."

He certainly had a really great three years under us. I think the system was set up for a guy of his skillset. He had a great senior year and fought his way to the NBA. When he was in the NBDL (what is now called the G League) in Huntsville, Alabama, he called me. He had been trying to get to the NBA, but he hadn't yet, and he said, "Coach, I think it's time for me to use the Notre Dame degree."

I said, "Matty, just finish this thing out. Just hang in there. Don't pull the plug on this yet. Just hang."

Well, a week later he got a 10-day contract with the Portland Trail Blazers. Then he got another 10-day. Then he got a 10-day with the San Antonio Spurs and he got a couple more 10-days. Then he was finally on a roster and eventually he signed the five-year, $25 million deal. So he always teases me. He says, "Thanks, man, for talking me off the ledge."

Jere Macura

I love Jere Macura. When Ryan Humphrey became eligible, the playing time of Macura and Ivan Kartelo changed from the year before. They both were really disappointed they weren't playing more. Kartelo eventually transferred to Purdue, and that was the right decision. Macura thought about transferring, too. I gave him his release, and he visited Northwestern. He came back and told me, "I don't want to leave."

I said, "You gotta talk to Swanagan." And Harold Swanagan loved him, so Jere stayed with us.

But I think it was hard because I didn't recruit him, and then Hump's presence changed the dynamics of his playing time. Tom Timmermans had come on the scene, too, and so those two other guys weren't playing like they were the previous year. I didn't want to burn a bridge because we may want to get another foreign kid. After Macura finished playing for us, he then played for a long time over in Split, Croatia, and he still is really close with Hump and Swan.

TORRIAN JONES

I loved the energy and athletic ability of Torrian Jones. He was always such a positive guy. At least he got to meet his coach before he got to campus, which was not the case with Chris Markwood and Tom Timmermans. Those two got to campus, came to their coach's office, and met me for the first time—a very unusual dynamic. I was still recruiting them. I told them, "Hey, I love you, saw tape of you." Torrian not only developed into a good player, but also a good coach. He's an assistant to Martin Ingelsby at Delaware, my former school.

CHRIS THOMAS

Matt Doherty had recruited Chris Thomas, and Chris had already committed to Notre Dame, and then we were able to keep him. He was such a gifted guy, and you could just give him the ball.

In February of my first season, I was still trying to recruit Troy Murphy a little bit to come back. But one day Murph—and this is when I knew he was gone—said, "Nah, Coach, you got that point guard coming in, and he's got the ball in his hands all the time. It's time for me to go." I walked out of practice that day thinking, *Yeah, he's gone.*

Chris was just very ready, very confident—sometimes a little overconfident—and a headstrong guy. When he was healthy, you look back at his clips, and he was really one of the most gifted players we've ever had. He got a triple-double in his first college game. It was the only triple-double in our history. He was just really, really good his freshman and sophomore years. The knee injury and the microfracture surgery changed that. I think he was a little frustrated he couldn't leave early. He thought he was a guy tracking that way. He came back for his junior and senior years while the guys he played against in the McDonald's All-American Game were in the pros already.

He didn't quite have the same pop and explosiveness, and so it was a more difficult junior and senior year for him. His stock was down NBA-wise because he was less productive. We laugh about it now because he felt so much pressure, but he carved out a very good European career, though he never could get to the NBA. He was a fearless kid who absolutely wanted to win, and there was a great toughness about him.

This was the first time I took a cell phone away from someone. It was the night before a game on the road when he was a freshman, and he had people hitting him up all the time. But there was a buzz around him because he was playing so great. I had him come to my room every night before a game on the road, and we would spend 20 minutes together talking. "I just want to see you," I said, "just want to check your temperature." He was a fearless dude and really gifted until that darned knee injury.

Jordan Cornette

Jordan Cornette had a great feel for the game. He was a great defender who just knew how to play. He was a big guy, was good with the ball, and could really defend. He wanted to be coached and he was kind of a flexible position guy. He could guard a center or he could get out and guard a point guard. It's amazing that he is our all-time leading shot blocker and he never blocked any into the second row. None of those blocks were highlight film versions. His blocks came when he'd get you from behind. He was just an amazing positional defender.

I remember we lost to Central Michigan here at the buzzer, and we were bleeding a little bit. We then had to go to DePaul the night they were naming the court after Ray Meyer. We needed a win badly, and he made five three-pointers in Allstate Arena to kind of stop that bleeding. He was the ultimate team guy. He was a rock solid college player and a great voice. It's not surprising he's in the media business now.

GREG BOSL

We played Purdue here on St. Patrick's Day in the first round of the NIT in 2004. It was the final game for Gene Keady, Purdue's head coach. We were winning, and the game was basically over. The final score ended up 71–59. I was already going over to shake Keady's hand and I yelled out to our guys, "Don't shoot. Just let the clock run out."

I saw Greg Bosl take two steps from his own foul line and launch it. It was a three-quarter-court shot and it went in. The crowd's going wild because of the difficulty of the shot, the victory against Purdue, and that it's St. Patrick's Day. But then I had to approach Keady. I said, "Gene, I'm really sorry."

JOHN CARLSON

Tyrone Willingham, the head football coach at Notre Dame at the time, had me meet with him on his recruiting trip. John Carlson's dad was a high school basketball coach. So the thought was maybe he would come to Notre Dame and play both sports. Very rarely does it work out they can play both, but we were banged up in 2003–04. The football season ended, and we had Carlson with us the rest of the year, and he played a little bit. He played in a CBS game at St. John's and did a really good job for us.

He played football the next fall, and that's when the coaching change was made, and Charlie Weis was hired. But Weis wasn't here much initially because his New England Patriots were in the Super Bowl. Carlson said to me, "Coach, I'm ready to come back."

I said, "John, you can't play anymore."

He said, "What are you talking about?"

I said, "John, you have a new head coach. You need to get down in the weight room. And you're going to have a new position coach. So you can't play basketball anymore."

He said, "Are you serious?"

I said, "John, there's just no way. I love you, I'd love to have you, but you can't do it. It was great last year. But now you've got a new coach. You can't be playing basketball when your new coach is looking for you in the weight room in January and you're on a road trip at Georgetown. That's not going to work."

I saw him about a week later. He said, "Thanks, Coach. That was good advice. You were right."

But he gave us a really good year, and it was neat having him around. And his dad still works our camp.

DANNY MILLER

Danny Miller was a key mercenary for us, maybe the ultimate mercenary. When we first heard of him wanting to leave Maryland, my assistants said, "Why would we take a guy for a year?" I thought about it for a couple of days and I came back and said, "You know what? One year is one year. With what we're losing, I think we need to invest in him."

His Maryland team went to the Final Four in 2001. But they had a lot of depth, playing time was difficult, and he wanted a change. Fortunately, I really knew the family well because Greg, his brother, played for me at Delaware. So we were able to get him in here, and he was sitting out when Ryan Humphrey, David Graves, and Harold Swanagan were about to leave. So I was losing three men who were really big-time players.

When Miller got eligible, we had a 23-year-old fifth-year guy. So we were old again in 2002–03. We would play small, and he would be the four man. Torin Francis was a freshman, and we had Chris Thomas, Matt Carroll, and Chris Quinn. That was a heck of a group. That's the group that won the BB&T Classic, beat Marquette early, and beat three top 10 teams in a week. That was fabulous.

After we reached the Sweet 16, he was so ready to move on with the next phase of his life, and it wasn't a negative at all. It was just who he was. He had his car backed into a parking spot. After his last final exam, his stuff was packed. He walked out, got in his car, and drove to New Jersey. He said, "Just send me the diploma" because he was a fifth-year guy and he was doing the European thing and the NBA from there. Our guys still laugh about that. Danny was just fearless, and I'll never forget him playing so well against Maryland that year.

TORIN FRANCIS

Torin Francis was a big guy who was maybe surprising for us to land because we hadn't done enough yet. It came down to North Carolina, Florida, and us—and Florida was rolling back then. Assistant coach Anthony Solomon did an unbelievable job with him. I did think his mother saw that our campus was a little smaller, a little more protected. His high school coach, David

First, was very involved. Plus, he was going to start. I told him, "You go to Florida, but you may be the fourth big guy. You're going to play 30 minutes here and start."

He came in, and that was one that maybe gave us some credibility in recruiting early because we hadn't really crushed it yet. His path was very similar to that of Chris Thomas. His first year and a half was like a buzz saw, and then he had back surgery. He was a little different after the back surgery.

Torin was also a guy who was looking and thinking maybe he could come out early. In that climate he would have come out and he would have been a first-round pick. But he decided to come back and then he got hurt.

He played his junior and senior years, but a little like Thomas, he was laboring. He was really picked apart by the pros. We really worked hard to keep his head up and keep him concentrating on team goals. Yet I was very conscious that there were guys who had potential NBA futures but never got there because of some bad luck physically. But he's still playing and he's carved out a really smart niche playing overseas. Right now he's in South America.

Francis played on that team of our former guys that won the championship in The Basketball Tournament, an alumni event. That was really a neat experience, going back with those guys. I went up to Boston University to the championship game and I sat across from the bench and cheered. The officials were Big East guys, so they were coming over to me, and I was working them a little bit. I was trying everything.

Those guys won the game and the $100,000, and I jumped over the press table. We had a great dinner the night before the final game, and then the night after they won it all, it was crazy. It was such a great tribute to how they felt about their experience at Notre Dame that they would come back and play together. Kieran

Piller, one of our former walk-ons, put the team together. Jordan Cornette and Ryan Ayers played great. Francis was part of that group and he's still playing and still doing his thing.

Chris Quinn

Chris Quinn was the first kid I recruited for Notre Dame, the first guy who committed under my watch. He was growing up in Columbus, Ohio, at the time, and Ohio State certainly wanted him. But they wanted to redshirt him, and that helped us. Then later I found out that not only was he Catholic, but there was also a picture of him on our basketball floor when he was four years old with his face painted.

Once we got him here on campus, I felt we had a great shot. He had lived in Chicago previously and grew up watching former Duke guard Chris Collins play in high school. That was his hero. The Quinn family got to know the Collins family, and the Quinns would be at Collins' Duke games. So when I saw Quinn's dad at a recruiting event in Fort Wayne, Indiana, I thought, "I know this man." But it's one of those things where you can't really talk to the family or it would be a recruiting violation; you kind of run by them in the bathroom and you introduce yourself. When I finally realized who this was, I said, "That's your son? Well, you have a scholarship. I will call you tomorrow." And so Quinn was the first guy. It was really neat.

Jim Boeheim, the Syracuse head coach, saw Quinn play after we signed him and said, "What are they gonna do with him? They've already got Chris Thomas." The answer was we were going to play them together

Quinn just had a great feel for the game, a great basketball IQ, and a great skillset. He was a better athlete than people thought. He had kind of a heartbreaking senior year in 2005–06 when we lost all those close games, including four in overtime. We couldn't get over the hump. He had the ball a lot at the end, and we just couldn't make a run.

But he got into the NBA and he was just a really steady player. Pat Riley loved him with the Miami Heat. He could be the head coach there someday. I had talked to Chris about becoming an assistant at Notre Dame. So when I ran into Miami head coach Erik Spoelstra, whose father, Jon, is a Notre Dame grad, Erik said, "Coach, you had everybody nervous."

I said, "Yeah, I thought it was a long shot, but I had to check it out first."

And Chris was great. He said, "I really thought about it, Coach, but I'm on this NBA track."

And I said, "I know, I know."

He coached the Heat summer league team in the summer of 2017 that Zach Auguste played on. He's really good. It was neat to follow him with the NBA, and they love him there in Miami.

Tom Timmermans

I can remember like yesterday when Tom Timmermans came in to meet his new coach the very first week of school. Those were very unusual circumstances. I'd heard about him. I just never saw any of these guys—Torrian Jones, Chris Markwood, or Tom Timmermans—on the circuit.

But Timmermans was great. I think he was just so pleased to be here at Notre Dame, so honored to have the opportunity to play here. He was patient. He knew we had some big guys who were going to play ahead of him. He just continued to hang in there and then really gave us some good stuff as he got older. Timmermans was a really physical guy; he was so strong that sometimes it would be misconstrued. But if you bounced off Timmermans, you felt it because he just was a rock.

We still kid about the game at UCLA. We went out there in 2004. The Bruins were having a tough year, and we blew them out. We played great in Pauley Pavilion, and Timmermans made a couple of three-pointers and had 20 points. It was his best game ever—he was the player of the game against UCLA on CBS. Dick Enberg, God rest his soul, referred to him as the "Dutch oven" because his shooting was so hot that game. So we always kid about that, "How about the 'Dutch oven' in Pauley Pavilion that night?" He was a great kid to be around, and I think he had a great experience here.

Rick Cornett

I don't know if Rick Cornett really loved the game when he first came here. But it grew on him to want to be a better player, and I think he realized that he could make some money maybe playing a little bit. In his junior and senior years, he really gave us good stuff.

He was always very quirky with his diet. Sometimes he would only eat rice and hot sauce. But he was a gentle kid, a very sharp kid. He played in Europe one year but was really smart about it and kind of just said that's it. He was so secure with putting the ball down and moving on. He's a senior executive at Warner Brothers in New York City now. He's married, he's moving up in the company. When we play in New York, he always comes around to see us.

Colin Falls

A lot like David Graves, Colin Falls made a lot of clutch shots. He was just a big-time shot maker. During his freshman year, we thought, *Gosh, how are we going to get him in the game?* And then it became, *Boy, we can't take him out.*

I'll never forget evaluating him at the Peach Jam Tournament. You could meet with high school juniors, so I drove to Chicago around April or so—and I think he felt I was going to offer him. But I didn't offer him. So I think there was a little tension there, but I told him, "We want to watch you some more."

Well, there's no spring AAU, so it wasn't until the summer that we saw him. I went to watch the first game in the Peach Jam, and he was absolutely rolling. So I was kicking myself that I didn't offer him three months earlier.

I walked out of the gym at halftime and I tracked down Larry Butler, who was the general manager of the team. I said, "We want him. He has a scholarship. Please make sure Colin knows that."

At that time I couldn't talk to or text these kids in the summer like you can now. I couldn't even call his dad at home. Once we were permitted to talk to them, I said, "Colin, I think you've been waiting for this and I want you to consider this over the next couple of days. I'm going to go back out on the road again Thursday for this next recruiting weekend. I could really change my plans if I knew you've committed, and it would really shape the class. No pressure. I'm not saying you have to. I'm not saying I'm going to pull it off the table. But you would really help me, and I could go chase some other guys."

And so the next day he called and committed.

He played a lot as a freshman in 2003–04 because he was a shot-maker for us. He hit maybe one of the biggest shots ever, and it wasn't for a championship or anything. It was to just make the Big East Tournament. Back then only 12 teams made it. We played DePaul here at home in our regular-season finale in 2006. We were teetering. If we lost that one, we wouldn't go to the Big East Tournament. And if you don't go to the tournament, the natives are a little restless. Colin had played through plantar fasciitis almost the whole year. We ran a set, and he caught the ball really deep in front of our bench and banged down a three to give us enough to win that DePaul game by five. We got to the Big East Tournament that year when we really needed to do that. So I always remembered his big shots.

He made a huge one against West Virginia as a freshman at the Garden in the Big East Tournament. The Mountaineers went to a 1-3-1 zone, Chris Quinn found him, and Falls made the three with 15 seconds left. We defended their last shot to win it by one. He made another big three with about four seconds to go against Seton Hall in 2005, and we won by one.

He was just a clutch guy and really a great captain. He was one of those guys, like Martin Ingelsby, who you could meet with and talk about the team. Falls and Russ Carter were two extremely different personalities in that 2006–07 senior class.

RUSSELL CARTER

Russell Carter was a guy we got on late; he didn't sign early. I went out to watch him between the Big East and NCAA Tournaments. He was really scoring the ball. He was built like a defensive halfback, like a linebacker really. He was a really sharp kid from Paulsboro, New Jersey. So we decided to bring him in on a visit.

He's the only kid who I've ever picked up at the airport who came off the plane with his own basketball. He had a special workout ball. He was a total gym rat. He showed me that ball when I was at his high school gym. It had a couple of sayings written on it. So we offered him, ended up getting him, and, boy, he really could score it. He was first-team All-Big East as a senior, but his play was mercurial at times.

One of the big games for us where we really needed a quality win was when Alabama came in here and was ranked No. 4 in December of 2006. It was a snowy night when Luke Harangody and Tory Jackson were freshmen. It was a blackout night where everybody at the game got a black T-shirt. We had not been to the NCAA Tournament in a while, and this was Year Seven. So this is where we needed to go back to the tournament, or it would have been four years in a row to the NIT.

We'd just beaten a ranked Maryland team on the road and we needed something else. And Russell made clutch shots that night, but they were the kind where I was saying, "No, no, no! Yes, yes! Great shot!" He hit two of those where he was rising up early in the shot clock. We were up six with three minutes to go. He was just on fire, though. He had 27 that night, and we ran off 14 points in a row over one stretch. He had another game like that in the 2007 Big East Tournament against Georgetown where he hit five threes and just went off.

He ended up playing in Europe. He's out in Los Angeles now, doing well and spending a lot of time working guys out. He stays in touch and really carved out a very good career with us after signing late. He was one of those guys, kind of like Matt Farrell, where we took him late, and it became a really good story.

DENNIS LATIMORE

Dennis Latimore was our transfer from Arizona, and you know who really helped us get him? Josh Pastner. He is now the head coach at Georgia Tech but was a manager at Arizona with Lute Olsen back then and Pastner really felt that we would be the best place for him. Oklahoma and Kelvin Sampson were really recruiting Dennis hard, but he ended up coming up here with us.

He was really an artsy guy who was into poetry. His readings on campus at Notre Dame would pack the house. He was a Renaissance man, he really was. And if you look at his numbers, he was pretty solid for us. We probably had a hard time playing him and Torin Francis together; it wasn't great spacing. But he sat a year, played a year, gave us some good stuff, and then had another year left.

But we got to the point where Rob Kurz was starting to develop and we really were going to invest in Kurz. And very matter of factly, I sat down with Dennis. He had a year of eligibility, but he was graduating. And I said, "Dennis, you can come back. I love you. But I can't guarantee you're going to be playing the minutes you played this year because we're going to really invest in Rob Kurz and some of these other young big guys." And he called me the next day, and he said, "Coach, you know, you're right. I think I'm going to move on."

He's now the head coach at Chino Hills in California at the school where the younger Ball brother started—and he won a state championship in 2018. He asks for coaching advice. I've sent him the offensive tape of the stuff we do, and anytime we've been in Los Angeles, he comes to see us and stays in close touch with all our guys. What was neat about him was that he really enjoyed the whole Notre Dame educational experience.

Omari Israel

Omari Israel was a Rockville, Maryland, guy, a D.C. guy. We really invested a lot in him. He played for the D.C. Assault AAU team, and we had been trying like heck to get a guy from that program—and we finally did. He was a great kid from Our Lady of Good Counsel High School.

It got to the point where it was going to be Russell Carter or Omari playing, and what has always won out in our program was whether you could make a shot. Omari got a little bit logjammed and decided to go where he could really play, and I thought it was a great decision. There was no animosity; it just made sense. We couldn't get him the minutes, and so he went to Loyola and had a nice run with Jimmy Patsos. But he still comes out here to visit, especially on football weekends. When he left it hurt a little bit because the D.C. Assault AAU team was down on us a little bit until we got Eric Atkins.

ROB KURZ

I'll never forget the first time I went to watch Rob Kurz practice. He was the starting center on his high school team, and the starting power forward was Matt Ryan, now the quarterback for the Atlanta Falcons. I remember their coach going, "This kid is going to Boston College as a quarterback." And then his AAU team was so interesting because he played with Kyle Lowry, who is with the Toronto Raptors and was a great player at Villanova. They only had six guys on that team. We watched them down in Orlando, and Kurz made every open shot from 15 to 18 feet and stuck his nose in there on every rebounding situation. I just loved him.

He committed when he visited in the spring. It was during the same time that Chris Thomas was announcing he was coming back after his sophomore year. So I was a little spaced out with all of these things going on. Assistant coach Sean Kearney brought Rob into the office and was about to take him to the airport. And I had no heads-up that he was going to commit to us. He must have told Sean on the way down the hall, but I was thinking *We're going to have to follow up.* So I was sitting with him and kind of wrapping it up, but I wasn't really concentrating because in 10 minutes we had the press conference for Chris and I was getting my thoughts together. I said, "Rob, I hope we made it clear how much we want you. I'll follow up with you later in the week."

He said, "Coach, I want to come to Notre Dame."

I said, "Oh, really?"

He said, "Yeah, I'm coming."

And I said, "You just made my day! That's awesome. Thanks a lot!"

And I walked out the door to the press conference, and Sean took him to the airport. That commitment was about as quick as it could be.

I just loved Rob's development. He had a real fight about him. The tough thing was that he came in here at 6'9" and 195 pounds, and then he broke his jaw. So his whole freshman year was a bit of a lost year. We got him back at the end of that first year in 2004–05, and that's when Chris Quinn got hurt in the Big East Tournament. We were right on the bubble. We finished the regular season 17–10. We ended up going to the NIT and we had Holy Cross at home. I was thinking we needed to kind of play for next year. So we didn't play Dennis Latimore except four minutes, and Kurz played 19 minutes and had 11 points. We lost, and I think there maybe were 1,000 people in the gym. But it was a message to Kurz because he was wondering, *Am I going to play here?* And I just wanted him to know in the last game of the season that, "Hey, we're investing in you. You're going to be our starting four next year."

And he became a real work ethic guy. He was a great leader. Luke Harangody came in and had all this fanfare as a sophomore and junior, but Kurz was a year older and really helped Gody become more mature and steady. He knew we needed Gody to win. When Gody was going to be the Player of the Year in the league, Kurz was the first guy to congratulate him. I thought it was really helpful to have the power forward who played along with Gody be a mature rock, someone who was little steadier psyche-wise, to help us through all things on the court. I'll always remember and always appreciate that about him.

Rob just became a great college player. He really did. He hooked on with the NBA for a year. But here was a guy who was very smart and knew when it was time to get out, and he's now a very successful businessman in Philadelphia.

Kieran Piller

Kieran Piller transferred to Notre Dame from Villanova; he did not come in as an undergrad. But he was one of the best walk-ons we ever had. He was so good with our guys, especially Russell Carter. He always wanted to talk hoops and he always wanted to know more. I always felt he'd want to be back around the game. After going to law school at Notre Dame, he's now an agent at Priority Sports. Piller was the guy who put together the alumni team in 2014 for The Basketball Tournament.

Kyle McAlarney

I'll never forget the first time I saw Kyle McAlarney in the basement gym at Howard University at an AAU event. At halftime I walked by Tony Sagona, his coach, and said, "We want him."

And Sagona said, "Done deal."

We just felt he was a great fit, and I think he wanted us. It wasn't hard to recruit him. A lot of people were getting in on him, including North Carolina State, but he knew he was a fit here, and we were able to get that done.

Another guy who made himself a player by being a gym rat, he had great toughness. He was a lot like Matt Farrell. They're very, very similar guys. Their personalities, toughness, stubbornness, they had an edge about them. McAlarney was a guy who had outrageous numbers, just crazy scoring numbers. He was the leading scorer in the state of New York for a while. He broke everybody's records.

So now we had that weapon in our style of play again. He really became a heck of a college guard for us and had some big nights. Against Syracuse in 2008, he made nine threes, which was a Notre Dame individual record. Then he made 10 of them the next fall against North Carolina in Maui. He was just a fearless, tough guy. I felt for him his senior year. That was the year we played the A schedule in the Big East, and we just couldn't get over the hump and ended up in the NIT.

But I loved the way he came back from his suspension. Everyone respected the heck out of him for coming back. He's one of those guys like Martin Ingelsby, who feels kind of like a son. He played in France for a while and now he's a high school coach and athletic director at his alma mater. He was a pleasure to be around. I miss that thick New York accent.

LUKE ZELLER

Luke Zeller was a big get for us because he was Indiana's Mr. Basketball and a McDonald's All-American. So we got a great player in our own state. It was between Notre Dame and Stanford, but at the end of the day, he wasn't going to go all the way to California. Certainly, the academics played a big role. Luke was very religious. He isn't Catholic, but the fact we had a strong faith-based operation here was very powerful for him.

I felt for him because we could never get him to his full potential. It's one that I look back on and say, "I wish I could have done a better job with him." I feel like I had unfinished business with him, and yet his attitude never changed. His work ethic never changed. He just kept plugging and trying. And he loves Notre Dame. He ended up playing in the NBA a year with the Phoenix Suns. He was just a special guy and he's so supportive of the program. He loved his time here and stays in close touch with his teammates.

RYAN AYERS

Ryan Ayers was such a steady guy for us. I loved his bloodlines since he was a coach's son. Even though he lived in Philadelphia then, he was kind of a Midwest guy because his dad, Randy, used to be the Ohio State head coach.

He and his mom came in for the visit because his dad was busy with the Philadelphia 76ers. During his visit Ryan said to his mother, "Mom, did you see that? There's a Meijer."

Assistant coach Sean Kearney and I looked at each other and thought, *What the heck?*

But it was almost like he was back in familiar territory because he remembered seeing Meijer stores in Columbus, Ohio. So I think he liked the idea of coming back to the Midwest.

His dad knew me, and I think he felt good about sending his son to play for us here. But the whole Midwest thing seemed to make things really comfortable for him here. He was a key guy for us even as a freshman because he was a freshman when Russell Carter was a senior. If Carter was having one of those mercurial nights, we'd play Ryan.

During the NBA All-Star break, we played at Cincinnati. Ryan came off the bench and hit four three-pointers, and we won.

His dad was able to be at the game behind the bench. I always felt good that he came to the game and got to see his son play well. Ryan had a heck of a career for us. He had a great basketball IQ, was a big-time scorer, and was a good shooter.

That class of Kyle McAlarney, Luke Zeller, Zach Hillesland, and Ryan Ayers was a special group of guys. They all committed in that first spring when you could bring juniors in on official visits. It happened Wednesday after Wednesday for four weeks. It was crazy. We were going, "Well, it's Wednesday. We're getting another one." They are all mature, dependable, smart, and team guys. They were really a neat group to be around.

I remember having Ryan in the office when he was a junior and saying, "Are you thinking about coaching?"

And he said, "Well, yeah, but first I'm going to play a little bit."

I said, "I get that. But you really should think about coaching. I know you've been around your dad, and maybe you don't want to do that, but I think you're a natural."

We talked about that conversation when I was hiring him here. He did a great job at Bucknell and he's a really gifted young coach.

Feeling the Burn

IT WAS A BIT OF A COMEBACK YEAR FOR US. WE WON A GAME AT Villanova in late January when the Wildcats were ranked in the top 20 and beat a ranked Marquette team at home a few weeks later. We beat George Mason in Denver in the first game of the NCAA Tournament and then lost to Washington State in the second round. They kind of put it on us and really guarded us. It gave us a clue for what Virginia would eventually look like because Tony Bennett was coaching Washington State then. We couldn't score on them to save our lives.

But at least we came back and won a game in the tournament. After three years in the NIT, we got back to the tournament the year before, but we lost our first game. We won 14 league games in 2007–08, and that's great any year in the Big East. All four of our conference losses were to ranked teams, and all of those were on the road—Marquette, Georgetown, UConn, and Louisville. Maybe the most impressive thing about that year was that we didn't lose at home for the second full season—and we kept that streak going until late January of the next year. We won 10 straight from late November into January and we played well enough to get ourselves back in the polls in February and March.

2008–09 (21–15, 8–10 Big East)

NIT: W 70–64 vs. UAB, W 70–68 vs. New Mexico, W 77–67 vs. Kentucky, L 67–59 vs. Penn State

Big East Tournament: W 61–50 vs. Rutgers (first round), L 74–62 vs. West Virginia (second round)

Starters:

- G   Tory Jackson, Jr., 5'11", 10.6 points
- G   Kyle McAlarney (captain), Sr., 6'1", 15.0 points
- G   Ryan Ayers (captain), Sr., 6'8", 11.1 points
- F   Luke Harangody, Jr., 6'8", 23.3 points, second-team AP All-American, first-team All-Big East
- F   Zach Hillesland (captain), Sr., 6'9", 4.6 points

That turned out to be an unbelievable season for the Big East because the league got three No. 1 seeds in the NCAA Tournament bracket. Pitt was No. 1 in the East, Connecticut was No. 1 in the West, and Louisville was No. 1 in the Midwest. We started the season ranked in the top 10 and had three eventful games early at the Maui Invitational. We beat Indiana pretty good in the first game there and then we knocked off No. 6-ranked Texas by a point. In the championship game, we lost to a No. 1-ranked North Carolina team that went on to win the NCAA title. Luke Harangody was tremendous with 29 points against Texas, and Kyle McAlarney hit 10 threes and scored 39 against Carolina.

We lost to nine ranked teams that year in conference play; those were nine of our 10 losses in the Big East. We lost five games in a row against ranked teams—Louisville in overtime, Syracuse, UConn, Marquette, and Pittsburgh. We lost seven in a row at one point, and what sealed the deal is when we lost at Cincinnati and flew right to Los Angeles to play UCLA, another top 20 team. We got our butts whooped in Pauley Pavilion, and that was seven in a row. We came back and we were pretty much written off by everybody, even though we ended the streak by beating No. 5 Louisville by 33 at home. We found a little bit of life down the stretch, but it just wasn't enough to get in the dance. We lost by seven late in the year at UConn when they were No. 2. But I loved the fact that we accepted the NIT bid and we got back to New York. We won three games in the NIT before Penn State beat us in the semifinals at Madison Square Garden.

McAlarney, Ryan Ayers, Zach Hillesland, and Luke Zeller were seniors. As disappointed as they were about not making the NCAA Tournament, I was really proud that we rallied. We talked about, "Hey, man, let's get back to New York City." When we got beat in the Garden in the Big East Tournament, I knew we weren't going to the NCAA. We were 17–15 at that point. I said, "Fellas, we're going to get an NIT bid. Let's try and get back to this building. That's who we are. We need to accept that." And they did.

We had three home games in the NIT, starting when we won at the buzzer against Steve Alford's New Mexico team. Tory Jackson went coast to coast against the Lobos to win in that second-round game. Kentucky came up here in an NIT game, and it turned out to be Billy Gillispie's last game as UK head coach. It was a circus here because that was the first time Kentucky had not been in the NCAA Tournament in 18 years. There was a great deal of conjecture about Gillispie's future, and he was let go two days later. We beat Kentucky by 10, and it was the last game in our arena before the renovation.

2009–10 (23–12, 10–8 Big East)

NCAA South Regional: L 51–50 vs. Old Dominion

Big East Tournament: W 68–56 vs. Seton Hall (second round), W 50–45 vs. Pittsburgh (quarterfinal), L 53–51 vs. West Virginia (semifinal)

Starters:

G Tory Jackson (captain), Sr., 5'11", 9.6 points

G Ben Hansbrough, Jr., 6'3", 12.0 points

G Tyrone Nash, Jr., 6'8", 7.8 points

F Luke Harangody (captain), Sr., 6'8", 21.8 points, third-team AP All-American, first-team All-Big East

F Tim Abromaitis, Jr., 6'8", 16.1 points

We had some really good wins that season, beating West Virginia, Pitt, and Georgetown when they were all ranked. But we were a game over .500 in the league, and then Luke Harangody got hurt at Seton Hall. It was February 11, and we lost by three that night in Newark, New Jersey, and that put us at 6–6 in the league. So we put Carleton Scott into the lineup, and that was the birthplace of the "burn."

Here's how the burn originated. Our first road game without Harangody was at Louisville, and we were sitting around as a staff after our team meal. We were talking about how to play without this major scoring force. Assistant Anthony Solomon started talking about when he was at Virginia and the Cavaliers played Houston in the NCAA Final Four. I said, "What was the score of that game?"

He said, "We lost 49–47 in overtime."

And I said, "Fellas, don't you think we just really have to slow it down and limit possessions?"

We hadn't practiced it, but we had two really good guards, Ben Hansbrough and Tory Jackson. So at the shootaround the next day, I said, "You know what? I want you to just run offense. I want us to burn the shot clock until single digits, and when we get to single digits, I want somebody, one of our big guys, to come set a ball screen for either Tory or Ben and let them make a decision."

We lost by two in double overtime to Louisville that night, but we played our butts off. We had four people foul out, but Tim Abromaitis had 29 that night in Freedom Hall, and Hansbrough and Jackson combined for 40 points. Jackson played every minute, and Hansbrough played all but two. Then we had the bye week and we were starting to play that way for good. Pitt came to South Bend ranked No. 12, and we beat the Panthers by 15. But our scores now were in the 50s and 60s.

We were burning, and it took on a life of its own. That's all anybody wanted to talk about. It became a psychological advantage for us, too, and our guys really believed in it. We played that way and we won four in a row to get us to 10 league wins. Then came the biggest dilemma. We'd won three in a row, and Carleton was playing great. We were burning. We had momentum and we didn't think Gody was ready to come back for maybe another two weeks. Then Gody texted me on the bus to Milwaukee to play Marquette. I'll never forget that because it was the most tied up in knots I've ever been as a head coach. He texted me from the back of the bus and wrote, "I'm ready. I can help up there tomorrow. I'm ready to play."

Well, we were playing pretty well without him. We were winning, and Carleton was helping us. So for about three hours on the bus, I'm wondering, *Okay, how do we manage this one?* We pulled into the hotel in Milwaukee, and I immediately said to Jackson and Hansbrough, "Come up to my room right away." It was a Friday before a Saturday afternoon game. And it was their team; they were running it. I said, "Guys, the big fella is ready to go."

And they both said, "No problem with us, Coach, as long as he defends. He's got to guard people."

I said, "I feel you, I hear you. I promise you he will."

They said, "We're good then. Let's move forward."

So I didn't start him. I brought him off the bench, and he gave us some good minutes. He scored five points and played 11 minutes. And we won up there in a crazy game. Hansbrough tipped it out to Scott, who made a shot to tie it just before the buzzer in regulation, and we won in overtime. It was a thrilling win. It was our 10th league win, and we were a lock now for the NCAA Tournament.

We were bussing back to campus, and I was thinking, *Okay, Gody is going to want to start.* So we headed to the Big East Tournament but still brought him off the bench against Seton Hall, and he played great, recording 20 points and 10 rebounds. We defeated No. 16 Pitt by five points the next night and then we ended up losing to West Virginia by two in the semis. So we had a great stretch there in New York. And my staff was right—we should have started him.

Then we were headed to the NCAA Tournament to play Old Dominion in New Orleans. I thought to myself, *Maybe we should start him now*. But the group that had started had won six of seven and they were playing pretty well. My staff said, "Start Gody," but I said, "We're going to stay the course." And my staff was right—we should have started him.

We couldn't really burn because Old Dominion played zone against us. What was crazy—and disappointing to me—was that it was an 11:30 AM tip local time. I was kind of excited, thinking this was in New Orleans, a big Catholic town, and there would be a lot of Notre Dame people. But there was nobody there. It was a horrible atmosphere. But credit Old Dominion. That team played great. We tried to get Gody back in there, and it was one of those games where, as I was coaching, I was thinking, *It's almost as if this group has run its course.*

We had maxed it out just to get the bid. The whole game was just hard, and nothing came easy. Old Dominion played loose, had nothing to lose, and deserved to beat us. So it ended there in the first round, which was disappointing, but when you think back, I loved how we figured out how to get there without Gody. There was nothing left in the tank at the end. We had pushed all the emotional buttons. But the burn was a great story in terms of getting there.

2010–11 (27–7, 14–4 Big East)

NCAA Southwest Regional: W 69–56 vs. Akron, L 71–57 vs. Florida
State

Big East Tournament: W 89–51 vs. Cincinnati (quarterfinal), L
83–77 OT vs. Louisville (semifinal)

Starters:

G   Ben Hansbrough (captain), Sr., 6'3", 18.4 points, second-
team AP All-American, Big East Player of the Year

G   Scott Martin, Sr., 6'8", 9.7 points

G   Tyrone Nash (captain), Sr., 6'8", 9.5 points

F   Tim Abromaitis (captain), Sr., 6'8", 15.4 points

F   Carleton Scott (captain), Sr., 6'8", 11.2 points

We had all these interchangeable parts in 2010–11. Everybody
was the same size. We didn't get to work with them until school
was back in session, and so there was a day in early September
when we were practicing. The assistants were all on the road,
so it was just me. I had Ben Hansbrough, Tim Abromaitis, Ty
Nash, Carleton Scott, and Scott Martin running through our stuff
without any defense. We really know how to play and we're all the
same size. I'm going, "Ooh. They're all big, we can pass, we know
when to screen."

That's when I really felt good about this group. The assistants
came back, and I said, "Fellas, you know me. I'm not one to get
ahead of myself, but this group is really interesting."

Hansbrough was driving the train with his flat-out toughness.
He grabbed us all by the throat, including me. After our team
meeting, he came down to see me. He said, "Coach, I think you're
selling us short."

I don't know what my tone was—maybe it was about just
getting to the NCAA Tournament. I wasn't talking about going

to a Final Four or winning it. If I was a younger coach, I might've been insecure if a player questioned me. But now I was getting excited about it. I thought, *Oh, my God, this is good. This guy's going to drive us.* Cincinnati head coach Mick Cronin said to me, "I came out before the game to watch Hansbrough. I was scared to death. He's almost growling out there."

Hansbrough just had an unbelievable edge. He was the Big East Player of the Year. There were lots of Hansbrough stories. We were playing Kentucky in Freedom Hall in the SEC/Big East Invitational. He had been an SEC guy at Mississippi State so he really wanted to play against Kentucky. He started off the game firing from deep and was making shots and scoring the ball. But they were not great shots; he was just playing on emotion. So he shot the fourth one from way out there and missed, and I didn't say anything. And then he shot the fifth one and missed again.

Then came a free-throw situation. We had gotten an offensive rebound, and Ty Nash was shooting a free throw. So Hansbrough was standing in front of our bench, and the free throws were down at the other end. So I got up but kept my hands in my pocket. My demeanor was calm, and I said, "Hey, Ben, maybe we swing the ball a little bit now. Those were deep ones early, so maybe we move it a little bit."

And he turned to me and he said, "Screw that. I'm rolling."

So I turned around, sat down calmly, and then I turned to my assistants and I said, "We'll revisit that later."

There are moments where you don't heighten the drama or stir the pot, and that was one of those, but that's what I loved about him. His eyes were always *that* big. I tell that story at clinics sometimes, and people just laugh. But that was Hansbrough.

We were a smart team. God, we were smart. We gave UConn that loss in the last regular-season game and played fabulous there in Storrs. Hansbrough became the Player of the Year in the Big East instead of Kemba Walker from UConn. And, of course, UConn went on to win it all and didn't lose another game after losing to us. But it was a heck of a group. We beat Akron at the United Center in Chicago in the first round of the NCAA Tournament. We were a No. 2 seed, and you could argue we should have been a No. 1. We won 11 of our last 12 in the regular season and won 14 league games. We didn't lose at home all year.

Then Florida State guarded the heck out of us in the second round. They were a No. 10 seed, and nobody had guarded us like that in the Big East. We just got frustrated and couldn't hit a shot. We couldn't score, and it was disappointing because that team could have gotten to a Final Four with the right breaks. I've had two teams that were good enough to do that—that year and then in 2014–15.

It was an unbelievable group to coach because they were old. Hansbrough drove the train. They were men every day. Nash had a great senior year. You had Martin and Abro; we only really played seven guys. Jack Cooley and Eric Atkins came off the bench. That was a neat group.

2011–12 (22–12, 13–5 Big East)

NCAA South Regional: L 67–63 vs. Xavier

Big East Tournament: W 57–53 OT vs. USF (quarterfinal), L 64–50 vs. Louisville (semifinal)

Starters:

- G   Scott Martin (captain), Sr., 6'8", 9.5 points
- G   Eric Atkins (captain), So., 6'2", 12.1 points
- G   Jerian Grant, So., 6'5", 12.3 points
- G/F Pat Connaughton, Fr., 6'5", 7.0 points
- F   Jack Cooley, Jr., 6'9", 12.5 points

Tim Abromaitis should have been a great story. He was our senior captain, he already had his degree plus an MBA, he was preseason all-Big East, and he had just played in the World University Games that summer. Then he tore his ACL the day after Thanksgiving. So Jerian Grant and Eric Atkins had to take over the team. They were in their second year, and those were two really good guards. They kind of set the tone for us. Pat Connaughton was in there, too, as a freshman, and we still had Scott Martin doing his thing. Jack Cooley was second-team all-Big East and was also the Most Improved Player that year in the Big East.

That was the year we won in double overtime down in Louisville when the Cardinals were ranked No. 10. That was a great win for us down there; we held them without a bucket in the overtime until the final horn. That was also the year we beat Syracuse here when the Orange were No. 1. The night before the game we showed a video of all the games where Notre Dame knocked off No. 1 teams. And then my guys went out and did it themselves.

We got back to the NCAA Tournament, went to Greensboro, North Carolina, and were up 10 on Xavier in the second half but just couldn't finish. And that was after watching Duke—the No. 2 seed in our bracket—get beat by Lehigh before us. We were thinking the bracket was opening up and then we couldn't get it done.

2012–13 (25–10, 11–7 Big East)
NCAA West Regional: L 76–58 vs. Iowa State
Big East Tournament: W 69–61 vs. Rutgers (second round), W
    73–65 vs. Marquette (quarterfinal), L 69–57 vs. Louisville
    (semifinal)
Starters:
   G   Eric Atkins (captain), Jr., 6'2", 11.2 points
   G   Jerian Grant, Jr., 6'5", 13.3 points
   G   Scott Martin (captain), Sr., 6'8", 7.9 points
 G/F Pat Connaughton, So., 6'5", 8.9 points
   F   Jack Cooley (captain), Sr., 6'9", 13.1 points, first-team All-
      Big East

We had a heck of a year that season. We had a great win against Kentucky here in the SEC/Big East Challenge when the Wildcats were No. 8 in the polls. Then there was the five-overtime Louisville game that we won here. I talked about it being a 15-rounder and taking punches and being put on the mat. At the fourth or fifth timeout, I said, "Has there ever been a 20-rounder?" It was a magical night and everybody had to be a part of it. Jerian Grant hit three threes at the end of the regulation when it looked like we were done. And Garrick Sherman ended up being a huge key and he didn't even play in regulation. This past season in 2017–18 when we went overtime with them again, Louisville coach David Padgett was pretty funny. During the second overtime, he said, "You want to play five?"

I said, "Maybe we should."

We won 25 games and we were a No. 7 seed in the NCAA Tournament in 2012–13. We had a great group, but we drew Iowa State in Dayton, Ohio, and the Cyclones just devoured us. That was the most upset I'd been after a loss in some time because I thought they broke our spirit. We hung our heads. They really treated us like the JV, and I think we were all embarrassed by that performance. It was just a sad way to end a pretty darn good regular season. We got to the semis of the Big East Tournament again. We kept getting to Friday night, but we could never get to Saturday.

Fred Hoiberg was the Iowa State coach, and the Cyclones were old. They just thrashed us. I felt really bad because Jim Nantz and the A crew were doing the game for CBS. I'm sure they went to another game quickly because ours was not very good. That one stuck with us for a while. Even in our spring workouts the next year, I was after our guys because of that game.

From the Big East
to the ACC

I REMEMBER VIVIDLY BEING IN JACKSONVILLE, FLORIDA, FOR THE Big East meetings with our athletic director Kevin White in 2003. This was when Boston College, Miami, and Virginia Tech were on their way out. At least that was the word. You could just feel the tension in those meetings.

Media were hanging out everywhere, wanting to know what was going on. Mike Tranghese, the Big East commissioner, was very uptight. He purposely had Kevin and Jane White at his table for every event because I think he was hoping Notre Dame would bring football and save the league. It was a last desperate effort, and Notre Dame was a key player in all this.

Kevin grabbed me and said: "Let's take a walk on the beach." And then Kevin said, "Let me ask you a question. Could we ever be independent in basketball again?"

And I said, "Let me think about that."

But I immediately thought that it would be hard to not be part of a conference now and be able to recruit. I think those days of being an independent are over for the sport. How would you get TV exposure? Would NBC hook us up like the old days and do some basketball? And who officiates our game? But it was very important for Kevin to keep our football independent and to maintain that brand. We got through that and we stayed the course in the Big East.

Then the next wave of expansion came, and we were really feeling it coming hard. We were at league meetings again in Jacksonville during the summer of 2011, and I was walking back from dinner with Jack Swarbrick. I think he was really getting pushed by people to bring football and come to the Big Ten. He was visibly tight—just like Kevin was. It was like a rerun. Just like Kevin, he was thinking: *Where do I put the rest of my sports here because we aren't giving up our independent status in football?*

We were playing in Greensboro, North Carolina, in the NCAA Tournament in 2012. It was the year we lost to Xavier in first round. And it was kind of percolating out there that something might happen with Notre Dame and the ACC. So John Swofford, the ACC commissioner, and his staff were running the Greensboro site for the NCAA. Swofford did the initial meeting, and as we were walking out, he grabbed my arm and said, "I'd like to keep you right in this league. You know that, Mike?"

I said, "Commissioner, I'm on the same page with you."

When we see each other now, he'll laugh and go, "You remember how I grabbed you after the tournament meeting in Greensboro?"

There were ACC posters up everywhere in Greensboro because they were the host. I remember grabbing one of them and I turned to Swarbrick and said, "What do you think?"

Joining the ACC was fortunate on two fronts. One, the ACC was a little worried about losing Clemson and Maryland—or maybe North Carolina State or Florida State. The rumors were all over the place. We were fortunate that we were able to come in and give the ACC some football games. We really landed on our feet.

Jack had always said the ACC is where we needed to land. That's what we were working. But as the Big 12 rumors kept going a little bit, the ACC knew we might have another option. Never in my wildest dreams did I think—while coaching at Notre Dame and in South Bend, Indiana—that I would be coaching back in the ACC, a league that I grew up a fan of, that I coached in. It was just amazing.

The day we announced it, we actually had a head coaches meeting. I went to Jack and said, "I'd love to go with you to the press conference." And he said, "That's awesome. You've got to come."

They knew me in ACC country, and so I was down there talking to all the media I remembered from my days coaching at Duke.

It was just an unbelievable win for Notre Dame. I thought Jack and Father John Jenkins, our president, did a fabulous job. Nathan Hatch, the president at Wake Forest and Notre Dame's former provost, got a huge amount of credit for working behind the scenes on the other presidents. And I think at the end of the day, Kevin White at Duke and Bubba Cunningham at North Carolina, who are both former Notre Dame administrators, were very, very supportive of us, and thought that we would add something to the league.

For me, personally, it was really exciting. It was rejuvenating in that the ACC was a league I respected and loved. I knew the programs and the bluebloods. You could get a little stale after 13 years in the Big East and with your preparation. It was like taking a new coaching job without leaving because you had new things to sell in recruiting.

What I've always tried to do is educate our fans that we're not independent anymore. We've only been in a conference since the mid-1990s and we changed leagues. So rivalries and everything else have been a little unusual. In those independent days, we had to hang our hat on whether we could upset the No. 1 team. And that was awesome, and it still is. But then we had to focus on league standings, league championships, and double byes. This was all new.

Becoming a respected program in a league like the Big East and the ACC was the goal, and it was really cool to see us get there. In our Big East days, we had many double byes and top-four finishes. We got to the Friday semifinals a lot, but we could never get to Saturday night. We, though, were a very respected program in the Big East. In fact, when they put the mini-conference together for TV purposes, we were in it. It was Notre Dame, Connecticut, Pitt, and Syracuse. From the mid-to-late '90s, we went from kind of being the whipping boy of the Big East to where we're part of the mini TV conference.

But it broke our back a little bit twice. We were 9–7 in league play in 2003–04 and 2004–05 and couldn't get into the NCAA Tournament. Then in the ACC, we started 6–12 in the league that first year in 2013–14 after we lost Jerian Grant, and it was like, "Uh-oh." And then over the three years after that, we became a really respected program in the ACC—just like we were in the Big East.

One of the most gratifying things to me is we have the respect of our league members and that the league can count on us to deliver and be there and carry the flag for the league and be in the NCAA Tournament pretty regularly. That was the case in the Big East and now in the ACC.

Going into our sixth year in the Big East—and my first year at Notre Dame—I'll never forget my first fall when Tom McElroy from the Big East office came out to meet with me and my staff. We were talking about the league. McElroy said, "Mike Tranghese is really waiting for the Notre Dame ship to come in." He was kind of implying: "We got you in here. Could you deliver for us a little bit?"

We had it going during my first year. We were barreling down the stretch and we were going to win the Big East's West Division. There were a couple of officiating issues I wanted to make points on with the league office. After a game we lost, I remember telling McElroy, "Hey, Tom, we're bringing the ship in. Can my man help me dock this baby now?"

He said, "I got you, man. I got you." I said, "We're doing our part. I remember what you said."

So I was really proud of that division banner. I knew how much Tranghese and the Big East wanted us to be a major player in the league. I thought we gave them great games, great runs, and some great Big Mondays.

Between the Big East and the ACC, we have probably played on Big Monday, ESPN's college basketball showcase, more than 30 times. Our program has been good enough for them to want us to be out there, and we've been a good story. But when you play on Big Monday, you're not playing the second division. I said one time that I felt a little like that movie scene with Rocky Balboa and Apollo Creed where the guy says, "Just give us a good show."

The summer before the 2017–18 season they told us, "ESPN really wants you guys. You've got Bonzie Colson and Matt Farrell and you've got a great story." So we got thrown in there a lot, and it affects your league strength of schedule.

I think we earned respect in both leagues based on what you'd hear from the commissioners and the veteran coaches. Guys like Roy Williams and Mike Krzyzewski told me a couple of years ago, "You guys have been a great addition to the league."

I have been so very fortunate at Notre Dame to work for two great athletic directors—and two very different people in Kevin White and Jack Swarbrick.

White was so interactive. He would always come by and say, "How's the best coach in America?" He would find me after a loss and say that. He took it all very personally. He hurt for you when your team got beat and he knew basketball because he had sons, including University of Florida head coach Mike White, who coached and played basketball.

I always knew this was Kevin's dream job. I knew how passionate he was about Notre Dame. We were both very new, as he was hired only a couple months before me. There were a couple of times when we'd go out and speak to alumni groups together because we were the two new guys. His passion for the place and that this was his dream job really came out. Kevin would travel with us some, too, and he was really supportive. He was always worried about his coaches, asking us, "How are you? Are you doing all right? Are you okay? How's your energy? You get some rest tonight."

He was just awesome like that, he really was. I vented to him many times, and he would sit there and listen. I sat in my office once and was so frustrated about where we were in the season and how our program was perceived that I threw a water bottle, and there's still a mark on the wall from it. I remember saying to him, "We're such imposters." I think we were just going through a tough stretch. And he would be amazingly supportive in those situations.

We became really good friends, but he absolutely took losses hard. During the years we just missed the NCAA Tournament, he was hurting even more than I was. I thought we should have gotten in the NCAA Tournament after we'd played the A schedule in the Big East and went 9–7. But we didn't get in. I remember saying to him, "How come you can't be on the NCAA Basketball Committee?"

And White, who was involved with the Bowl Championship Series Committee, said, "Well, there's no way the Notre Dame athletic director will ever sit at the BCS table and the NCAA Tournament Committee table. That's too much."

Jack and I developed a bond in part because when he came in he knew I had been here a while, and he liked how we ran the program. We immediately talked a little bit about the lay of the land. And we got really close. We've become really good friends through it all because we went through the complications of all the turmoil with the league. We'd discuss all the basketball stuff, how to improve. So I've really enjoyed that aspect of our relationship. Jack has a feel for the big picture of college basketball, and we're always kind of sharing ideas on that. What I love about him is he never panics. He's always been very steady, puts it in perspective.

One of the greatest pieces of advice I ever got from him was at halftime of the Northeastern game in the 2015 NCAA Tournament. I was maybe a little tight, and the game was close, and he caught me at halftime and said, "Be Five-Overtime Mike, please." He was referring to the five-overtime game we played with Louisville a couple of years before when we just sort of let it rip. And I thought, *That's pretty good. He really knows me.* And I think he appreciates our style. He likes being around our program.

I've really been lucky. I've had two great athletic directors. I've had two great presidents. Monk Malloy, our former president, was a D.C. Catholic League guy, so we always had a connection. Father John has been amazingly supportive, and he and I have gotten closer because we were meeting regularly on the

Rice Commission that he was on. So I was spending more time helping get him more educated on college basketball. It's been neat to connect with him on this because these are the kinds of conversations about our business and the philosophies of college athletics that you might not have every day with your president.

At Notre Dame I've had really supportive guys, enthusiastic guys who wanted to help, but they're also guys you could become friendly with. And yet they could still be your boss. They were in charge, but you could actually be yourself with them.

13

Triumph in the ACC

2013–14 (15–17, 6–12 ACC)

ACC Tournament: L 81–69 vs. Wake Forest (first round)

Starters:

- G   Eric Atkins (captain), Sr., 6'2", 13.9 points
- G   Demetrius Jackson, Fr., 6'1", 6.0 points
- G   Steve Vasturia, Fr., 6'6", 5.0 points
- G/F Pat Connaughton (captain), Jr., 6'5", 13.8 points
- F   Zach Auguste, So., 6'10", 6.7 points
- C   Garrick Sherman (captain), Sr., 6'11", 13.5 points

OUR FIRST YEAR IN THE ATLANTIC COAST CONFERENCE WAS THE year we lost Jerian Grant at midseason to the academic suspension. His last game was right before Christmas against Ohio State at the Garden in New York, and we kind of blew that one at the end. Ohio State was really good—the Buckeyes were ranked third— and we lost by three. Maybe that was a little foreshadowing of what was to come. Not only did we lose like that, but I also had to officially tell the team that Jerian was not coming back with us. He got on a train and went home to Maryland because he was out of school. Talk about just feeling crummy.

I was worried. But our very first ACC game was at home, and we beat Duke by two. Eric Atkins and Pat Connaughton played fabulously in our victory. It was a great memory that our first ACC game was a win against Duke when Jabari Parker was a freshman. It was a heck of a thing. But we just didn't have enough going forward. Certainly, Grant was a huge loss. Down the stretch we played great at North Carolina in the last regular-season game but lost 63–61.

But the worst thing that happened was that our bye week came the last week of the season, so we had to wait nine days before we played Wake Forest in the first round of the ACC Tournament, which was our first time there in Greensboro, North Carolina. I was very disappointed in the 81–69 loss. We didn't compete at the level we needed to. We were beaten down. Jerian was there that day; we got him tickets. He was sitting right behind the bench. We went back to the hotel, and I was not very happy. I said, "I want all the returning guys up in my room after the meal. Eric and Garrick Sherman, you seniors, I don't need you. I'll get with you when we get back. I want the returning guys."

Earlier that week I had Grant come to my room. I said, "Look, when you come back to school, I don't want you feeling guilty." I went through all that with him. And so now they were all in the suite area of my room, and I was still thinking about what I wanted to say to them. Then I walked around the corner, and Connaughton had his arm around Grant. And I thought to myself, *That's powerful right there.* I still get goose bumps when I think about that because we were at a little bit of a crossroads, and that was pretty damn good. I kind of talked about the fact that we had slippage in our culture, slippage in our standards, and that it was not acceptable moving forward. We were not going to have Grant back until June, and Connaughton was going to go play baseball that summer. So we were going to be broken up a little bit.

That's when we brought in Dr. Joe Carr to do some sports psychology stuff with our group. I just thought we needed it. Demetrius Jackson had had an up-and-down freshman year, and I thought we had work to do. We did some really intense sessions in the summer and aired some stuff out, and the staff really challenged me on some stuff. We got a lot out on the table, and I wanted to create the right culture going into that next season because I thought we had a chance to be good.

2014–15 (32–6, 14–4 ACC)

NCAA Midwest Regional: W 69–65 vs. Northeastern, W 67–64 OT vs. Butler, W 81–70 vs. Wichita State, L 68–66 vs. Kentucky

ACC Tournament: W 70–63 vs. Miami (quarterfinal), W 74–64 vs. Duke (semifinal), W 90–82 vs. North Carolina (championship game)

Starters:

G   Jerian Grant, Sr., 6'5", 16.5 points, first-team AP All-American, first-team All-ACC, ACC Tournament Most Outstanding Player

G   Demetrius Jackson, So., 6'1", 12.4 points

G   Steve Vasturia, So., 6'6", 10.1 points

G/F Pat Connaughton (captain), Sr., 6'5", 12.5 points

F   Zach Auguste, Jr., 6'10", 12.9 points

We came back together and went to Italy on a foreign tour in August. We had Pat Connaughton, Jerian Grant, Demetrius Jackson, Zach Auguste, and Steve Vasturia. And I was watching our group and thinking, *We know Grant's pretty darn good, but now there's Connaughton setting the tone, too. These guys, it's their team, and they're seniors.* Jackson was more comfortable as a sophomore and he was a great talent. Vasturia was just so steady, and Auguste was starting to come around. We didn't play great competition over in Italy, but I was getting excited about our team. Some of the culture rebuilding we did looked like it had helped. Dr. Joe Carr even traveled with us at times through the year. He came and checked in with us and he had everybody's cell phone. He was great with me, too. He was another guy I could talk to as a sounding board.

A lot of the same language we used that summer, we use here now. *Raincoats, power claps, kills.* That was Carr's language from the summer. The raincoats are symbolic of when a teammate challenges you on something. It means you can take it, you don't get defensive, and you let it roll off your back. Power claps defused frustration from a bad play, a foul, or a problem with a call. Instead of dwelling on it, we all power clap at once and then move on to the next play. It worked to reset us. We always used to do a drill at the end of practice called three stops. Carr introduced a kill, which means three defensive stops in a row. We still keep track of that. In a timeout I often refer to how many we have or don't have. If you could get to double digits in a game, that was through the roof. A lot of times we'll end practice with a half-court drill where the first team to get a kill forces the other team to run. It's a good way to end on a competitive note. We made T-shirts that said "Raincoats and Power Claps" and wore them as shooting shirts.

We played in the Hall of Fame Tipoff event in Connecticut and beat UMass and then lost to Providence in the championship game. Bonzie Colson was a freshman, and I didn't even put him in a game. I was feeling a little guilty about it because his family was all there, and he didn't get in either game. We beat Michigan State by a point in overtime in the ACC/Big Ten Challenge, and that was a great confidence-booster. That was a win that made us believe a little bit. We won 11 in a row after that Providence loss and we kind of got it going.

We won every close game. We beat North Carolina down there in early January. We were still kind of the newcomers in the league then, and so Connaughton still remembers my pregame speech before the Carolina game. I said, "You do know that Carolina didn't want any of you. You may have gotten a token letter, but they did not really think any of you were good enough." Pat told me later, "That was great, Coach, that you said that." Auguste defended a three-point shot; he switched out on a guard, and the Tar Heels shot an air ball, and we won it. To win in Chapel Hill in just our second year in the league was unbelievable. We were starting to feel like we belonged.

We beat Duke here at home—they were ranked fourth in the country—and then we got smoked at Duke down there about a week later. But we were in the hunt late for the regular-season title in our second year after going 6–12 that first year. What a great bounce-back year it was.

We went to Greensboro, North Carolina, for the ACC Tournament, and it ended up being one of the great accomplishments in the history of our basketball program. To win it by going through Duke and Carolina on Tobacco Road is really awesome. At the Friday night semifinal, we had Duke beat with about 50 seconds to go, and 85 or 90 percent of the arena was walking up the steps early because the crowd was all Duke. The next night we had Carolina down, and it was 90 percent Carolina fans, and they were all leaving. I was used to ACC Championships when I was an assistant at Duke where the whole building was there celebrating with you. We only had our group right behind our bench. It was a fabulous memory and it was amazing how well we played in those two games.

In the Carolina game in the championship, we were down nine. We came out of a timeout and just got on a roll. And there was one of the great offensive sequences in the history of Notre Dame basketball. We reversed the ball all the way around, and then Steve made a three in front of our bench to give us our first lead and we just took off from there.

I was a little bit in shock. I went up to cut the net and I don't know if our fans—or even our players—really understood the significance of an ACC Tournament championship. Growing up as an ACC guy, this was unbelievable to do it on Tobacco Road against these guys. We had the trophy out on the court after the presentation. Nobody wanted to leave the locker room. So we were all talking and celebrating, and Brian Morrison, who handles the media for basketball for the ACC, came in and said, "You may want this." He had the trophy because we had left it out there on the floor. I turned to him and I said, "We're new at this. We're trying to get a feel." Athletic director Jack Swarbrick had a great speech in the locker room. To celebrate that with our program on Tobacco Road, there's been nothing better in my coaching career than that. And we had great momentum for the NCAA Tournament.

Our first NCAA game was in Pittsburgh against Northeastern, and it was one of those teeth-gnashing games where we were having to battle. And I was tight as a drum. Jack had to remind me to loosen up.

The second-round game was Butler, and my mom died that morning. We were at the shootaround at Duquesne, and I had a message from my brother, Shane, when I got on the bus. He said, "Hey, man, call me when you get a chance." And he was great; he was so calm. He said, "Hey, look, Mom passed. I'm pretty sure it was her heart. We've got Dad; he's with us. We're good, so do what you've got to do."

We talked a little bit. I said, "I'll be there tomorrow, no matter what, all right?" That next day was also my birthday.

I thought about her a lot. I didn't think much about the game and was kind of reminiscing. But I was trying to get mentally ready because my guys needed me; we had a chance to maybe go to a Final Four. There were times that we came out of a timeout, the guys were going out on the floor, and I had a fleeting thought about my mother. Swarbrick and Jim Fraleigh, the deputy athletics director, knew, but I wasn't going to tell the team before the game. Zach got a big rebound late but then double dribbled. We had a timeout, and Jackson kind of went off on Zach. But that group knew itself so well, especially Grant and Connaughton, who went right to Auguste, and Grant went right to Jackson. They calmed it down, and we ended up winning in overtime, just a great win. Connaughton made an amazing block at the end of regulation.

I was in the coaches' locker room, a tight little room, before the press conference. And Jack said, "Are you going to tell the team?" And I couldn't do it. I said, "Could you do that for me?" So he explained it all, we went to the press conference, and Connaughton and Grant came up to me and looked like we'd lost the game. And I thought, *Damn. I want them to smile.* They were great, though.

They said, "Coach, are you all right? We've got your back."

I said, "Hey, man, it's all good. Mom had a good run."

That was maybe the most bizarre postgame scene I can remember in terms of just emotion. Nobody quite knew what to say. I was talking about the game during the press conference and I know I've got to come clean. I try to segue into it. I said, "There's probably something you need to know." There were a couple of writers working on their computers, and when they realized what happened, they came up front. It was actually neat to talk about my mom's career and who she was.

The university plane took me to Orlando, Florida, the next day, which again was my birthday. My brother picked me up. Wichita State and Kansas were playing, and we were going to play the winner of that game. My sister-in-law had a little dinner. They had a birthday cake. We were all there, including my dad, and I was thoroughly exhausted and kind of spaced out. But we had the family there. I told my nephews, "All right, you scout Wichita State, and you scout Kansas." We watched the game and grabbed something to eat. They drove me back to the airport, I arrived in South Bend at about 10:00 PM Sunday, and got ready for the trip to Cleveland.

We played fabulously against Wichita State. We were absolutely rolling. We had the look and we end up beating them by 11. We're just kind of on autopilot, just playing in all facets. Then we had a great matchup with Kentucky, and people still talk about that game. I think it still has a cable viewing record. I've run into the refs from that game, and they always bring it up, telling me it was the most amazing game they ever officiated. There was serious energy in the building. It was just a fabulous college game, and it was thoroughly disappointing that we couldn't win it because that was the team you really felt could win a national championship. I really felt that group had the look. Coming out of Greensboro, we were so confident. To this day I still get comments on that game and the high-level game that it was. Jerian couldn't really get the shot off at the end because 7'0" Willie Cauley-Stein ran right alongside him the whole way down the floor.

We bused back the next morning from Cleveland to South Bend. When we arrived on campus, I thought, *We've got to get one more picture.* So we walked down into the arena, and there was an ROTC basketball event going on, and all the kids gave us a big hand. I said, "Can I just get a picture at half court with these guys one last time?" Everybody was in sweats, and it's a really cool photo. I just needed one more picture with that group because that was the last time we were together. We were kind of frazzled from exhaustion and travel and everything. But it was an unbelievable memory and just a fabulous year. I remember hearing stories about our fans at the team hotel kind of taking over the lobby after those two games in Cleveland. Our whole group was having a great time all night, like it was never going to end. It was neat.

Both Grant and Connaughton were back on campus for the Texas football weekend that next fall. We had a recruiting dinner Friday night at Ruth's Chris Steak House, and I thought we would do something special there. The guys had no idea we'd do this, but we showed a highlight video to give us a little recruiting punch, and at the end, I got up and said, "We haven't ordered you any actual food for dessert, but I actually have some of my own dessert to present." We had six of the waitresses come out with silver platters, and each of the platters had their rings. That's how we delivered them their ACC championship rings.

2015–16 (24–12, 11–7 ACC)

NCAA East Regional: W 70–63 vs. Michigan, W 76–75 vs. Stephen
F. Austin, W 61–56 vs. Wisconsin, L 88–74 vs. North Carolina
ACC Tournament: W 84–79 OT vs. Duke (quarterfinal), L 78–47 vs.
North Carolina (semifinal)
Starters:

G   Demetrius Jackson (captain), Jr., 6'1", 15.8 points,
second-team All-ACC
G   Steve Vasturia, Jr., 6'6", 11.4 points
F   Zach Auguste (captain), Sr., 6'10", 14.0 points
F   V.J. Beachem, Jr., 6'8", 12.0 points
F   Bonzie Colson, So., 6'5", 11.1 points

We were absolutely going to celebrate winning that ACC championship by hanging a banner. My thought was to do it the night of the first game on November 13 against St. Francis and then move on. We really started the process back in the summer. I talked about creating a new identity and about "being poor" again. Psychologically, I found I was better off by saying to people, "Yeah, we lost two great ones, but we've got a good nucleus coming back." That helped me when you had all these people congratulating you. It helped me turn the page.

Our guys really got in a mind-set that they wanted to show they could be great without Jerian Grant and Pat Connaughton. That's what's neat about different teams. As much as they loved Grant and Connaughton, they were already a little tired of hearing, "Well, what are they going to be like without those guys?"

They had a great challenge, and once we dropped the banner, it was official. We set the theme of moving forward with our players and staff back in the July workouts. We were hungry again.

In our first three practices, we went back to some of our basic stuff that we did as we were building the previous year. Whether it was coming off a 6–12 conference record one year or 14–4 the next, we were doing the same three defensive drills. We were right back where we were before in terms of building it again. We had to act like we were poor again; that was kind of the theme.

I wanted all my focus on my relationship with Demetrius Jackson and Zach Auguste. I needed to have tunnel vision with these guys. The leadership part was my biggest concern moving forward. We tried to groom Jackson, Auguste, Steve Vasturia, and even Austin Burgett as a senior. Could Martin Geben and Matt Farrell be guys to help us more? Bonzie Colson was efficient playing 18 or 19 minutes the previous year, but could we use him for 30-minute stretches? We were still trying to figure out how to play with him as the second big guy because he didn't stretch the floor the same way Connaughton did. V.J. Beachem was a junior, and we needed to get him confident again. We had a good track record of juniors delivering.

The bar was really high now, and our guys knew that. They wanted it really bad; sometimes I had to loosen them up a little bit. They were not resting on their laurels, but we had lost an NBA first-round pick in Grant and a second-round pick in Connaughton, two unbelievable warriors. And, quite frankly, I wasn't quite sure where our leadership was going to come from. I did not know if Jackson and Auguste could provide the leadership that our seniors had traditionally done such a good job with. I really give them a lot of credit for becoming better leaders than I thought they would. Vasturia was a junior and a rock, too.

But because of those question marks and departures, we were picked fourth in the ACC. We scratched out 11 league wins, which was good for a double bye. We beat Duke at the

Verizon Center 84–79 in overtime in the ACC Tournament in Washington, D.C. Earlier we had beaten Duke down there 95–91, and to win in Cameron was just amazing. It was really powerful. That's when Colson went off with 31 points, and Jackson was fabulous with 24. It might have been the best game he ever played in a Notre Dame uniform. It's still the only time Notre Dame has won at Cameron.

But we got down 12 or 14 in a home loss to Miami toward the end of the regular season. We only scored 50 points, and Jackson was kind of walking the ball up. I was thinking, *God, we've got to get it up the court.* So we played Farrell more and let Jackson get down the floor. And the last regular-season game against North Carolina State, we ran more and scored 89 points and won by 14. We were playing a little quicker.

We beat North Carolina by four here when the Tar Heels were ranked No. 1 and beat Louisville the next week, but Carolina smoked us in D.C. in the ACC semifinals. Farrell came off the bench in the ACC Tournament. So we talked about maybe starting him in the NCAA Tournament, even though he had not started a game to that point. I said, "I just really think that's the way to go."

But I got major blowback from the staff. Assistant coach Anthony Solomon was all over it. Slo said, "We should start Rex Pflueger because Pflueger's giving us good stuff off the bench."

I said, "I just think we need another quick ballhandler." We were still debating and arguing, and I walked to the door and finally said, "Hey, final decision. We're starting him. I don't want to hear anything more."

So we started Farrell in the NCAA Tournament. For the first week of the NCAA Tournament, we were in Brooklyn, which we kind of liked because we'd had some success at the Barclays

Center. Farrell's first start came against Michigan. He played really well for us, and I didn't even tell him he was starting until gameday. Then against Stephen F. Austin with the way the Lumberjacks pressed and played defense, we needed two ballhandlers. He was fabulous in that game. He was like pressure relief. And what a great win for us. Everybody in the building seemed to be cheering for Stephen F. Austin. We did a great job going two-for-one in the last minute to get an extra possession. Pflueger made the kind of play that he always makes because he has a nose for the ball. He made the tip-in right at the end to get us to Philly.

Then we had Wisconsin, a heck of a team, and it was another one where we were down and out. The whole tournament we were stealing wins. We were down double digits against Michigan and won. We needed the tip-in to escape against Stephen F. Austin. We were down again against Wisconsin, too. So we pressed, and the Badgers turned it over late. We ended up just stealing that Wisconsin game—literally. That was Demetrius making unbelievable plays at the end. We trapped, their kid tried to step through, and we stole it. And then as Wisconsin was coming down the court one last time, Jackson stole that one, too. We won by five and we had no business being in that game. Wisconsin fans in the building were going, "How the heck did that happen?" I mean we somehow just snatched that one. It was just a great win for us in Philly.

Then we had Carolina, who had just beaten us by 30 two weeks before in the ACC Tournament, in the Elite Eight. This time we played great. We made a little bit of a run in the second half. I thought we had it back. We got it back to one possession, but the Tar Heels had a little too much firepower for us and wore us down. Their rebounding, particularly on the offensive side, killed us. We couldn't keep them off the backboard, and they ended up winning by 14.

But we went to the Elite Eight again when we really probably weren't supposed to be in that territory. It was just a gratifying year. V.J. had a really tough postseason the year before, but this time he was voted All-East Regional. I also was really proud of Zach and Demetrius for their leadership.

2016–17 (26–10, 12–6 ACC)

NCAA West Regional: W 60–58 vs. Princeton, L 83–71 vs. West Virginia

ACC Tournament: W 71–58 vs. Virginia (quarterfinal), W 77–73 vs. Florida State (semifinal), L 75–69 vs. Duke (championship game)

Starters:

G Steve Vasturia (captain), Sr., 6'6", 13.1 points, first-team All-ACC Tournament

G Matt Farrell, Jr., 6'1", 14.1 points, first-team All-ACC Tournament

F V.J. Beachem (captain), Sr., 6'8", 14.5 points

F Bonzie Colson (captain), Jr., 6'5", 17.8 points, third-team AP All-American, first-team All-ACC

C Martinas Geben, Jr., 6'9", 3.1 points

Bonzie Colson was starting to really become our guy. Off the previous year's NCAA Tournament success, V.J. Beachem played great. And Steve Vasturia was his usual steady self.

Matt Farrell ended up the most unique guy early in the season. He was our most improved player. We won the Legends Classic in November in Brooklyn at the Barclays Center, and he made all the plays. People were saying, "Where does this kid come from? He was a three-star recruit."

We had a great makeup. We beat Louisville here in early January when the Cardinals were a top 10 team. We beat Florida State here by a dozen when the Seminoles were ranked No. 10. We lost 10 games but to a bunch of good teams. Nine of those 10 losses came to ranked teams. We were playing on the last Saturday at Louisville with a chance to tie for the ACC regular-season championship. If we had won and North Carolina lost, the Tar Heels would be the No. 1 seed because they beat us head to head. But record-wise, we would have gotten a trophy. At 12–6 we still got the double bye. And I was just so proud when we reached the ACC Championship Game again.

There are programs—long-standing ACC members—that haven't tasted the championship game in 30 years, 40 years. And we went to two in our first four years in the conference. And we won it in our second. It just gave us great credibility in the league and nationally.

I am still amazed at the Princeton win in the first round of the NCAA Tournament because we were exhausted. Colson was hurt, but somehow we escaped and won that game. We had nothing left in the tank for West Virginia's press, but that group made an unbelievable run. To be playing for the regular-season title on the last day and then playing in the ACC Championship Game, that was pretty good stuff, and it gave us lofty expectations for the next year.

From Harangody
to Grant

Luke Harangody

From Day One Luke Harangody gave us such a toughness and an edge. I'll always be very connected to Harangody and Tory Jackson because those guys came as freshmen and gave us a point guard and a big guy to get us back to the NCAA Tournament.

I remember seeing Gody play in Houston at an AAU event. I went down to see him in the spring and then met with him at the high school, but we didn't offer him initially. I saw him two months later playing another AAU event and I was thinking, *I can't believe I didn't offer him. I hope we can close the gap.*

So we offered him quickly after that. I met with him at school, and you knew he was not going to go too far from home. It quickly came down to Purdue and Notre Dame. His parents both went to Indiana, and his brother played football at Indiana, but it was Purdue or us. He was a Catholic kid who went to a Catholic high school, so I felt we had an advantage there.

Gody is the reason I learned how to text on the old flip phones.

I couldn't get him on the phone; he wouldn't pick up. He wasn't a man of many words. So my daughter Callie was sitting in our house texting on her phone, and I said, "Callie, show me how to do that." She gave me a tutorial on it, and so Gody gets some credit for me learning to text. That's how you could get him to communicate.

I always felt we were in good shape with him, but I could tell the needle was moving during a phone conversation after he'd already been up to campus a couple times unofficially. He said, "Coach, you have really good guys. I love your guys."

And that class of Kyle McAlarney, Luke Zeller, Zach Hillesland, and Ryan Ayers was indeed a great group. They and Rob Kurz were like brothers to him.

We were thrilled to get him. He was a little bit off the radar, even though he had a good spring. He committed to us before the summer and said, "Coach, do you have any problem if I don't want to do any AAU stuff and not go to the Nike camp in Indianapolis?"

I said, "Fine. What are you going to do?"

He said, "I'm going to work out with my brother."

I joked, "Fine with me. You're committed, and I don't want anybody else seeing you and maybe trying to get you to change your mind. You stay there in Schererville and hide."

So I think his ranking and all that stuff suffered because he didn't play the summer circuit. I was thinking he was coming in as a little bit of a prospect; maybe he needed a little time. But then we put him in for the first exhibition game, and he played about 15 minutes and had 14 points and seven rebounds. Assistant coach Sean Kearney and I were kind of giddy the next day. We were thinking, *Oh, maybe we've got something here.*

Zeller was still the starter, and the senior class then was Colin Falls and Russ Carter. But after about the eighth or ninth game, I said during practice, "Gody, turn it white," which meant I was going to start him. Falls gave me a look as if saying, "It's about time. Where has that been, Coach?"

We started him inside, and he gave us that anchor. He was so good against Alabama in that 2006 game where we needed a quality win. He had the ability to score. It's like in baseball how they say you need to be good up the middle. Well, we had Jackson's toughness up top and Gody's toughness down low. Plus, we had Kurz. Then it was great to see his progression and to see how he was able to step out and face the bucket and make three-point shots.

His game at Louisville in 2008—when he had 40 points, three three-pointers, and a dozen rebounds—was one of the great performances in our history and basically won him Big East Player of the Year honors right there. He had epic battles against Hasheem Thabeet and the UConn front line; he'd take those guys on and get 25. He became kind of this cult figure, and the TV guys loved Gody.

He got himself in great shape after he was a bit heavy, carrying some body fat his freshman year, though he still was productive. Once he was in spectacular condition, he was even more relentless. He suffered a knee injury his senior year in 2009–10, and we didn't think we'd get him back. The tricky dynamic was that we had Carleton Scott in there, and we went on a win streak and won a couple of games. He came back in the Big East and NCAA Tournaments.

He was going to go pro; he wrestled with it after his junior year. But he came back and unfortunately suffered that injury. I really respect what Gody did professionally. He tried the NBA thing a little bit, but he found he was a European guy. He's carved out a great niche professionally, making very good money in Europe. He knows who he is.

He had an unbelievable career for us. He's the second all-time leading scorer in Notre Dame history and he was at least in range of Austin Carr's record before he got hurt. I love the fact we started the Ring of Honor with Luke being the first one up there, and that's where he deservedly remains.

TORY JACKSON

Tory Jackson's recruiting was interesting because we didn't do much with him early—nor did we think we could get a point guard of his quality with Kyle McAlarney just one year ahead of him. We thought that'd be too close. So we didn't really recruit him.

During the first week of school in August, assistant coach Lewis Preston came down to my office and said, "Hey, would we be interested in Tory Jackson?"

I said, "Oh, my God, yeah, we'd be interested in Tory Jackson."

The word was that he was going to commit to Michigan. He was a Michigan kid, and I think he probably always envisioned he'd go to Michigan or Michigan State. But Michigan took another commitment instead of him, and I think Tory was a little taken aback by that. So we got a call from his AAU coach, and I said, "Absolutely we're interested. Tell me where I need to be."

Lewis and I went up and did a home visit in Saginaw, Michigan, where Jackson has a huge family of 12 brothers and sisters. The whole house was full, and his mother had some questions for us. But he had already visited, and we felt we were going to get a commitment. He ended up shaking my hand after his mom asked her questions and then he wanted to get out of there. Everybody was kind of in his face, and so I said, "I'll call you tomorrow." We stayed and had dinner with the rest of the family. He committed, and they were all very proud of him going to Notre Dame.

What I loved about him was his upbeat smile and energy. There was always that voice in practice and there was always that energy. T.J. Gibbs has that for us now. You just loved being in Jackson's presence because you couldn't beat him down. He had that robust laugh.

He was just a tough, tough guy. We were indebted to him because McAlarney was out of school that spring semester in 2006–07, and Jackson jumped right in as his replacement. We had one non-league game without McAlarney before the Big East schedule started, and the first five or six minutes Jackson was really shaky. I was thinking, *Oh, God.* Then he got into a rhythm, and we beat Louisville at home in our first league game. We ended up going 11–5 in the Big East with a freshman point guard.

During that freshman season, we had Russell Carter and Colin Falls on the wings, and they both wanted the ball and could score. Tory was a freshman and he was doing a great job. We were playing Georgetown in early January in our first league road game and we hadn't played away from home for a month. We lost, and it got back to me that Falls and Carter were chirping a little bit that Jackson didn't see them when they were open.

In the next team meeting, I ripped into all our guys. I said, "Look, this guy is a freshman. We're asking him to play 37 minutes, guard the best guard, run the team. You better be supportive of this guy and hold his hand and pump him up because basically he has saved us. He saved our season. We're an NCAA Tournament team because of him. So don't give me this stuff about he's looking guys off. If he's looking guys off, he's got dudes in his face or he's exhausted."

Both Carter and Falls were like, "Yeah, yeah, you're right, Coach." They were great with him after that.

Tory went on to have a great career. One of the great games I remember here is when we beat Syracuse his senior season, and he had 15 assists against that zone. He was cutting it up, throwing it down the middle, just probing it. He was slicing it up with his passing. I still share that tape of Jackson with our guards as a guide on how to attack Syracuse's zone. I have it archived.

JONATHAN PEOPLES

We took Jonathan Peoples out of St. Joseph's High School in Chicago. We had the utmost respect for that program and Gene Pingatore, a legendary high school coach who coached Isiah Thomas and so many more. We were over there looking at a big kid who was a junior, and Peoples was a senior that fall who was unsigned. I liked him, and we needed another guard to give us some depth at the guard spot. He really knew how to play, had a feel for the game, and could pass it.

So after about a week we went back, I offered him, and he committed. I liked getting a kid from that program at St. Joe; plus Peoples had a little different edge to his game. He gave us a lot of really good minutes. He started for a little bit until we put Tim Abromaitis in the starting lineup. But he was a really good utility guard who could do a little bit of everything for us. He made five three-pointers against Providence here in a home win in December of 2009 in one of his best performances. But he was a key guy who would come off the bench. He knew how to fit in and how to move the ball.

ZACH HILLESLAND

I went to watch Zach Hillesland at Toledo St. John's High School in Ohio, the day after we had a great win against UConn. I always liked to go recruiting after a big victory because you have a little more buzz when you're walking around. Hillesland was handling the ball, going up and down the court. I was with Ed Heintschel, who is a legendary coach at St. John's. I turned to him and said, "I think he's a guard. He's 6'8", but he's handling the ball."

He wasn't really shooting it that much, but he was bouncy, could run, and played above the rim. And he was great with the ball; he could handle or drive by people. Because we had four guys visiting together, I told him, "Zach, you could really start this thing going. You know the guys we're trying to get in here, you know the class we're trying to put together. We need one to get it started." He called me back the next day and committed. Hillesland was the guy who got the ball rolling. That's the recruiting class when we got commitments on those four straight Wednesdays.

Hillesland could guard a lot of positions, could handle the ball, could pass. He was just a really flexible guy. And he was a real believer in the program and the system. We used him in the middle of the press against Louisville in a game where we really needed a win. And he was coming down against the press and making plays and cutting people up.

It's been neat to have him as one of our radio guys because he's back around. And we still tell some great stories on the road.

TYRONE NASH

Tyrone Nash came out of Queens, New York, and we beat Kentucky out for him. I'm not known for my use of a deep roster, and when he was a young player, he came in my office once and said, "Coach, I feel like I'm the eighth man on a seven-man team." And he was.

I said, "Well, you got me."

I tried to paint a picture. I was trying to get him to hang in there and stay with us and not transfer. It was that old sophomore crossroads year we sometimes reach with guys. Fortunately, he ended up sticking it out and became a heck of a front-line guy for us. I called him my point center. We used to have him bring the ball up the court because he was a great ballhandler. And he was such a key on that 2010–11 team that earned a No. 2 seed in the NCAA Tournament. He was a man with that group—and very physical.

I loved his demeanor because he was always really calm. I used to call him "Smooth Jazz" because that's what he brought. He was really level all the time; he never got too anxious. He put together really great junior and senior years after hanging in there. It really worked out well. He has always been a classy guy, one of the best dressed guys we ever had on our team. He has played in Germany, France, and Israel and is still playing overseas.

TIM ABROMAITIS

I almost blew the recruiting of Tim Abromaitis. We started looking at him, but we didn't do anything. Then we started looking at him again in August. Assistant coach Sean Kearney sent me the tape and said, "This kid's interesting. What do you think?"

I thought, *God, he is interesting. Did anyone see him play?* Well, we didn't see him in the summer; he played on a different circuit.

Finally, we watched him work out and we liked his size, strength, and balance. He had lift and could shoot it. A bunch of good academic schools—William & Mary, the Ivy Leagues, and Yale because his brother was there—were in the mix. I was hoping he would agree to a five-year program where we could redshirt him. I thought that would be great, but I probably made the mistake of talking about it a little too soon, and it kind of cooled everything. But we were still working on him. We got him out for a visit, but he was very quiet.

But once again, one of the great selling points of our program has been our own guys, especially on official visits. You get around our players, and parents of prospects get around our juniors and seniors, and they see how they interact, and it's just such a powerful thing for, I think, all of our athletic teams. Ryan Ayers and Zach Hillesland brought him out of his shell a bit. Abro would just chuckle. He wouldn't say anything; the man never said a word. But he was the smartest guy we've had in the program. He was off the charts intelligence-wise.

His dad, who played at UConn, asked me about the redshirt thing. He said, "Coach, I've got no problem with that. But I just need to know: are you going to be here?"

And I said, "Jim, great question. It's my goal to retire here. I'm not going to mince any words. Hopefully, we can be good enough they don't fire me, and I can hang around here. I love coaching the kind of guys we've got. I think that's why your son's so interested in us. You've been around our guys and you've seen what we're about."

And so we ended up getting him. He and Jerian Grant were the youngest freshmen we've ever had. We ended up redshirting Abro the second year. And we made a mistake, interpreted the rule wrong, and played him in two preseason games, thinking those didn't count. Then he blew his knee out. But he bounced back from all of that and had a great career for us; he made himself into a pro prospect. I'm really proud how much he improved in our program. I think people back East and in New England were shocked at what he was doing here. They knew he was good, but they never thought he would have crushed it to the level he got it to.

Plus, he got his master's degree and did it all in five years. We actually tried to get a sixth year for him, and they initially denied it because of those exhibition games. It was our mistake, and that's such a shame for a guy who was the Big East Scholar-Athlete of the Year three times in a row. This wasn't a guy trying to beat the system.

At the end of his fifth year, I was on the board of the National Association of Basketball Coaches (NABC). NCAA president Mark Emmert was in the meeting with us, and the NABC executive director, Reggie Minton, brought up Abro's situation. Emmert's tone seemed to suggest that the situation probably could have been handled better. He looked at me and said, "Maybe you should submit his case again."

So I was very pumped and I came back to campus and called Abro in. I said, "Look, I think if we resubmit it, we're going get it this time. There's been kind of a public outcry."

And I'll never forget this. He said, "Coach, all my buddies are gone. I think it's time for me to move on. I had a great experience. I think it's time for the next challenge. All the guys I ran with are gone. I'm feeling kind of old around here now."

I thought about it, and he was right. We didn't resubmit it, and he is enjoying a nice, long career in Europe.

BEN HANSBROUGH

Ben Hansbrough just had an edge about him that you loved. On Hansbrough's recruiting visit, assistant coach Sean Kearney and I were in the Varsity Club having breakfast. His dad was here with him on that Sunday morning, and I think Ben had really connected with all our guys. So I said to him, "Where are you in your recruiting visits? What do you think and what's going on? I'd just kind of like to know so I can handle our business the right way."

He said, "Coach, I had a great visit. I think I'm going to visit Oklahoma State next weekend and then I'm going to maybe go to Southwest Missouri State the following weekend." He was rattling them off.

His dad interrupted him and said, "Hey, Ben, why don't you go upstairs and pack up, all right? I want to talk to Coach Brey a little bit here."

When Ben went up to pack, his father turned to me and said, "Coach, this will be one of the best decisions in Ben's young life. Give me two days. That's it."

I said, "Thank you very much."

Just as his father said, Ben called two days later and said, "Coach, I've canceled the other visits, I'm coming to Notre Dame."

Ben was still in school at Mississippi State during that visit. We had Scott Martin in to visit at that same time, and I think they kind of bonded as transfers. Those two were going at it in practice every day. I kept thinking, *I've got these two guys who are absolute men getting ready to get eligible for us.*

Once Ben was eligible to play, it was obvious there was that great edge about him, and he was really pushing us. With him and Tory Jackson in the backcourt, we had such great toughness. And it was that toughness, especially when we went without Luke Harangody for a while, that got us to the NCAA Tournament. Then his senior year in 2010–11 was one of the great stories of a kid coming from where he was to be the Big East Player of the Year.

He drove us and took us with him for an unbelievable ride. There were days when you wanted to punch him. But what helped him was that he had seniors with him that understood him. So when he'd get crazy, the rest of the guys were like, "Hey, let Ben be Ben." Because it worked on game night. He made it crazy in a practice, and I had some confrontations with him. But just the toughness, the fearless attitude, the edge about him—all that was so great.

Ben would be sweating and screaming before the game. Pat Holmes Jr. was one of our managers and was kind of his personal workout guy. We ended up a No. 2 seed in the NCAA Tournament, and Ben just wouldn't let us ever be soft. And it was such an old, mature group to work with. They just ran themselves.

He had an unbelievable Notre Dame experience. At the team banquet after his senior year, Ben's dad handed me a really moving letter. Those are the kind of things that make you feel you're doing your job as an educator. Ben publicly talks about Notre Dame and he still texts me about it. He misses it. He'd been a little bit all over the place, and his parents felt like Notre Dame got him a little more focused. He's doing commercial real estate right now in Tampa, Florida. I think he'd really be a bright coach and would love to see him get back into that field.

CARLETON SCOTT

Carleton Scott was an interesting guy because I never saw him play and he committed to Notre Dame without seeing the place. There have only been two of my guys who have done that—Scott and Elijah Burns. But we felt good enough about Carleton from tape and our eyeballs in Texas to know that he'd be a great fit in our program. You know who we beat to get him? My predecessor, Matt Doherty, who was at SMU at the time. They were probably going to get him.

I thought he was a redshirt candidate. He needed to grow, and I was really hard on him his first year. But Carleton grew up and bounced back and really became a good guy off the bench for us. Then as a junior, when Luke Harangody went down, he came in and was a key guy to get us to the NCAA Tournament.

After that strong year, he had one more year left and was talking about testing the waters. I loved him as a kid. He was special, but I think he maybe looks back and knows he should have stayed that fifth year. When I went to the Kentucky Derby for the first time, I got a call on Sunday coming home, and he said, "Hey, I need to talk to you." I got back and met him at the office. He said, "Coach, you know I'm really thinking about putting my name in for the draft."

I said, "Well, I understand. You know I do think you need some more seasoning."

He said, "Well, the one thing I'm worried about is: if I come back, I really need to be a three man. I need to handle the ball and play three."

Carleton ended up leaving, but I wish he had come back for another year. He has returned to work our camp. He's still connected to this place and his teammates. And I think he really had a great experience. He was one of those kids who just hung in there with us and got better. And he had that great run his last year.

Scott Martin

I just always knew Scott Martin fit how we played. I was really excited about him. I was out somewhere, and assistant coach Sean Kearney texted me: "Scott Martin leaving Purdue."

I texted back: "Jackpot."

I was really excited when we got Scott because I remember seeing him as an instate kid when he was in high school in Valparaiso. I always said he was a beautiful basketball player because of the way he just flowed and understood how to play. He was skilled and knew how to screen, move, defend, and give help. He was just so well-schooled. I just loved watching him play. I was really fired up when we got him, and he had three years left with us. Former Marquette coach Al McGuire used to talk about transfers and the wait before they could play and say, "I've got them in the freezer." So I'm thinking to myself, *I've got Ben Hansbrough and Scott Martin in the freezer. That's two pretty darn good guys to have in the freezer.*

As soon as we plugged them into our motion offense, it just flowed. Everything moved better when Martin was on the court. Our team defense was better when he played with any four other guys because he would talk and he would rotate and take charges. He got banged up a little bit, and we were always trying to keep him healthy. Like Tim Abromaitis, Scott suffered an ACL injury, which was really disappointing for Luke Harangody because they played together on the same AAU team but never got to play together at Notre Dame because of the injury. Gody was really busted up when he found out.

I was at Penn Station, a sandwich place behind the Starbucks on Route 23 near campus. I met Scott's parents there, and it was raining like heck. He had just sat out a year and now he'd blown out the knee, and they were just devastated. Plus, his dad was fighting eye cancer, so there was so much going on. We just tried to paint a positive picture. We did get him back, we got him healthy, and we got the sixth year approved for him.

He's carved out a nice niche playing in England, and I think he's going to be a really good coach. He's another guy on my radar.

ERIC ATKINS

Eric Atkins was a key guy for us out of D.C. We closely followed his AAU team, Team Assault, and his high school coach Pat Clatchey was calling me. I've known Clatchey since I was at Delaware, and he was calling me about EA when Atkins was in ninth grade. So we stayed on him and got in there early. EA lost his dad to prostate cancer when he was in ninth grade, but he and his mom were really drawn to Notre Dame.

He came out here unofficially for a game against South Florida. We were in the old arena, and our opponent was playing in practice gear because their uniforms didn't show up. And he was thinking, *Are they really in the big time? What is this?* He tells the story now, and we laugh about it.

But he knew. He knew if he came here, the timing would be right. Ben Hansbrough was a senior, so we needed EA to handle the ball as a freshman. He was the one young guy on that very mature NCAA No. 2 seed squad. We really played seven guys, and he gave us great steadiness. He just knew how to play basketball and could run a team. I always felt good—like when I had a Martin Ingelsby or a Chris Quinn—that I could communicate through him to the team. I've really been blessed with those guys as guards. They can sell the message on the court, in the locker room, and in the hotels. And EA was a pleasure to be around, just a steady guy with a really steady demeanor. There was a toughness about him, too.

One of the greats lines came from his mom at the end of his junior year. She said, "I've got to be the only parent in the country that complains that my son plays too much." He was playing 40 minutes every night. We never took him out. During his senior year in 2012–13, we went five overtimes in the game against Louisville. He played the whole game—50 minutes. Then we hosted DePaul three days later. We were understandably flat, had nothing left. And that one went overtime, and he was cramping up. I was ignoring him.

I was yelling at him, "Nope, you're finishing." He was dying, and I was going, "Nope, you can't come out. I'll give you three days rest after this one."

And he was looking at me like: "Coach, I'm all locked up."

Finally, Skip Meyer, our trainer, got him stretched out, and we ended up winning by four in the overtime.

It was crazy. Because of the five-overtime game, at one point his minutes in league play averaged 43 a game.

His senior year was our first year in the ACC. And in our first ACC game, he played great and we beat Duke by two. His buddy and former AAU teammate, Tyler Thornton, went to Duke, so that win was really big for him. We just didn't have enough juice his senior year without Jerian Grant to kind of hold on. But he played in the NCAA Tournament three times, and I loved how he paired with Grant. I called them my Baltimore-Washington backcourt.

EA was steady. I always knew he'd be a heck of a coach, and that's why he's on my staff.

JACK COOLEY

Assistant coach Gene Cross and I went to Chicago to watch Jack Cooley play for Glenbrook South High, and the team he was playing against was packing it in with this 2-3 zone. Cooley wasn't getting any shots, but he got every rebound out of his area. He grabbed everything with two hands, made every free throw, and got fouled a lot. It was halftime, and I said, "Where's his dad?"

Gene said, "That's him right there, walking into the concession stand."

So I got up, got in line, and got right behind his dad in the concession stand, and he turned around and said, "Hey, Coach, really appreciate you coming."

I said, "I want you to know your son has a scholarship from Notre Dame. I love him. I'll call you tonight."

And he responded, "Ah, ah, ah…I don't know what to say."

I said, "I can't talk to you. So go get your hot dog and get out of here. I just want you to have that message at halftime so you know how I feel. But I'll call you later."

Wisconsin was involved a little bit, but once we offered, we got in there quick. Cooley was very physical, very strong. I don't think he loved the game a lot when he first got here. It was a means to an end. He was a brilliant kid, and his test scores were off the charts.

As a sophomore on that 2010–11 team, he came off the bench. And as a freshman, he usually guarded Luke Harangody. So, of course, then the nickname "Little Gody" popped up, and Harangody was not real fond of that, and the players knew it. They used to tease him about his "little brother."

At one point during that year, I didn't let him guard Harangody in practice because Cooley was playing so physically. He was just beating the crap out of people. Harangody already was dealing with Hasheem Thabeet from UConn one day and then some big, physical guy from Louisville the next. So I said, "He doesn't need to deal with you today."

Jack had a really key sophomore year for us on that team. Then his junior and senior years were unbelievable. He was the Most Improved Player in the Big East as a junior. He was good with the ball and grew to love the game. The lightbulb went on, and he saw he could make a living out of it. And he's been really smart. I don't know if I've had a guy handle his professional career with better decisions. He was on the two-way contract with the Sacramento Kings in 2017–18.

JERIAN GRANT

It was neat to get a guy from DeMatha, my alma mater. Jerian Grant was part of an unbelievably gifted high school team that had Victor Oladipo, who played at Indiana and is now with the Indiana Pacers; Quinn Cook, who played at Duke and is now with the Golden State Warriors; and Jerian's younger brother Jerami, who played at Syracuse and is now with the Oklahoma City Thunder.

Jerian Grant was really young but very gifted. He had a real feel for the game, great court vision, and an ability to pass it. We were watching his AAU team with Oladipo and both Grant brothers. And we were also recruiting Oladipo, but we probably couldn't get them both. So I said, "Let's invest in Jerian. Let's really go after Jerian."

He visited UNC-Charlotte in the spring of his junior year, and Virginia Tech was sniffing around. Virginia was on him a little bit, too. You knew the bloodlines were good because his dad, Harvey, and uncle, Horace, had long NBA careers. The crazy thing is that he never really verbalized his commitment to me. After Eric Atkins committed, I was really focused on Jerian. Atkins had committed back in the spring, and now it was October. Tom Crean was there to deal with Oladipo because he had just committed to Indiana. Guys on the DeMatha team were committing, so now Jerian was feeling it. We were right there.

Virginia wanted him, and then it didn't want him. Then Virginia wanted him again. Providence really wanted him, but he wasn't going to Providence. I went to DeMatha, and Mike Jones, the DeMatha coach, said, "Come watch the workout. He's going to commit to you after the workout." The scouting service guys were already tweeting out: "Jerian Grant committing to Notre Dame."

Jerian's mother, Beverly, called me a week before and said, "What do we do to get him to say he's coming, Coach?" Seriously. She said, "Give me some advice. We're trying to get this kid to say he's coming."

So the workout ended, and there were a lot of coaches in the gym because DeMatha had all kinds of prospects. I wanted to get some private time with Jerian so I could get his personal commitment. Since I knew the layout of the school, I took him out in the hallway by the principal's office. I made small talk with him, kind of delaying. I wasn't getting anything. We talked for about five minutes. Finally, at the end I just said, "Awesome. I am so thrilled to coach you." Almost like he said it, but he never said a word. So I continued, "You know I'm going to take care of a DeMatha guy. This is going to be exciting, Jerian."

He was kind of going, "Yeah, yeah, yeah" but not really saying anything.

I said, "It's going to be great. I know a lot of scouting service guys want to talk to you. And, by the way, I'm going right up to Baltimore to visit with your backcourt mate, Eric Atkins, right now. I'm taking a car up to see him."

After I said that, he shook my hand, but he never actually said he was coming. It got out that night that he was coming and he had quotes like, "Yeah, I'm going to Notre Dame." But he never told me directly.

So at our banquet his senior year, I told the story and then at the end I said, "Jerian, would you please come up and shake my hand and tell me you're coming to Notre Dame?" And he came up and did, and everybody gave him a big hand. It was great.

Once Jerian did come, we had a pretty good team. We had guards, we had men. He was really gifted, but he was young. And he had a stress reaction in his shin that we were keeping an eye on. In his first exhibition game, he played seven minutes. He was beside himself; he wanted to transfer. Brad Brownell, the Clemson coach, called me because Jerian's brother was a senior at Clemson at the time. Jerian had called his brother and said he wanted to leave. Brownell was really classy about it. He called and said, "Hey, look, I'm just letting you know the phone call that Jerian's older brother got. I don't want to get into your business, but I wanted to give you the heads-up."

Harvey Grant, his dad, had redshirted, and his mom was worried about the stress reaction. But just seeing all his buddies play and him not playing was going to be a dagger for him. Because of the injury, we shut him down for about a month from December to mid-January. Right after that, we made the decision to redshirt. We had not talked about redshirting him at first. But with Ben Hansbrough and Scott Martin, I couldn't get him productive minutes and I did not want to burn a year of eligibility. The injury just kind of solidified the decision.

When we were down in Orlando, Florida, for the Old Spice Classic, which we won, ESPN's Dan Dakich was at practice. And Jerian was practicing really well. Dakich came up and said, "Tell me about Grant."

And I said, "Don't, don't go there." I was struggling.

He said, "What do you mean?"

I said, "We're redshirting him."

He said, "You can't redshirt him."

I said, "Oh, Dan, don't push me."

Dakich said, "You can't redshirt him."

I said, "No, he just agreed to it last week. Please, don't make me lose any more sleep. I saw the whole thing today, too."

Dakich and I kidded about that at the Maui Invitational in the fall of 2017.

In his second year, it was going to be Jerian and EA running things. And they were really ready to do it. Jerian had to go through the academic suspension and he took it like a man and came back. Thankfully, we did redshirt him because he had that year of eligibility to come back.

He came back as a senior, and there was not a better guard in the country. With the NBA guys, the consensus was he was the best guard off the ball screen his senior year. Along with Pat Connaughton, they grabbed the team by the throat again—the same way Ben Hansbrough did—and their teammates followed them.

15

Connaughton, Colson, and Co.

PAT CONNAUGHTON

We didn't start recruiting Pat Connaughton until late July before his senior year. Associate head coach Rod Balanis did a fabulous job keeping an eye on him as a junior, just knowing about him and staying plugged in. I didn't see him until late July. I immediately loved his toughness, fearlessness, and skillset, and we offered him right away.

What helped us with him was that it was evident that he wanted to play both basketball and baseball. He had a lot of other offers, but some of the other Power Five schools balked at him playing both. Balanis found out from his AAU and high school coaches that we needed to make sure he knew we were okay with him playing baseball. I had a conversation with his father, Len, and I said, "You know he's got an offer."

He said, "Coach, I just have one question. How do you feel about Pat playing baseball?"

I said, "Absolutely. We will work that out. He's a pitcher."

He said, "Coach, I really appreciate that. I'm pulling for you, you know, the Irish."

I said, "Well, we're going to get you out here for a visit, no pressure, and methodically go through it."

So we recruited him for basically six weeks, and he committed. And there was just an aura about him as a winner. He had an it factor. He rose up in big moments and had toughness and athletic ability.

We did a little Midnight Madness event his freshman year, and he won the dunk contest. He was very proud of that. He would talk about that even when he was a senior. So we saw this freakish athletic ability right away when he was playing for us as a freshman.

He was a great teammate. It was interesting how he and Jerian Grant bonded, even though they came from very different backgrounds. He became the 41st pick in the NBA draft and he's making his mark in the league now. It's just one of those really great stories.

His baseball path hit home for me because I'm a big Baltimore Orioles guy. I called him on baseball draft day and said, "What are you thinking?"

He said, "I don't know, Coach, maybe I'll end up with your Orioles."

And darned if it didn't happen. So I called him later that day. I said, "Hey, if you get tired of basketball, man, the Orioles could use you."

All my buddies back in Maryland grew up Orioles guys. They kept telling me, "We need your guy. He needs to play baseball. Get him out of basketball. He needs to come back. We need Connaughton. He's done with basketball."

Well, he's not done now because the 2017–18 season was a big year for him. I think he really would have entertained the baseball thing because the Blazers weren't sure they were going to sign him. They put off signing him for a month, but he finally signed in August 2017 and really became a solid NBA player. But if it doesn't happen, he can come back to the Orioles.

JOEY BROOKS

Joey Brooks committed to us really early, and we were excited about getting a kid out of Houston. He was athletic and could really guard. No one had more personality. He was the mayor of his dorm, very popular on campus, and just a great communicator. I think he had a hard time finding his confidence here as far as basketball, but his attitude was always good, and he hung in there, kept trying. He helped us win a couple of games off the bench.

When he was senior, we knew we had these other guys coming like Jerian Grant and Pat Connaughton. I sat down with Joey before the season and said, "I just don't know how much you're going to play. But I know you want to graduate from here."

We decided to redshirt him his senior year so that when he graduated he had the opportunity to go play his fifth year somewhere else. And he was really on board with that. He still was on the blue team every day, practicing and competing. At the end of it, he gave football here at Notre Dame a quick shot and then he decided he was done playing basketball.

He's on the Purdue staff now. I've talked to Matt Painter about him, and he thinks he's a bright young coach.

MIKE BROGHAMMER

The sad thing about Mike Broghammer is we could never get him healthy; those knees just gave out. We felt for him. He was a physical power forward who tried like heck to get healthy.

He fought in the Bengal Bouts, an intermural boxing fundraiser, his senior year and got to the championship round. We happened to be playing at Marquette, and the boxing championships were on a Friday night. We got into the hotel, and we timed it so we could do our team dinner and Mass and then pull it up on the screen and watch him fight for the championship.

He was on a medical hardship as far as basketball by then, but he was boxing. He didn't win that final bout, but our guys were all fired up to watch him.

TOM KNIGHT

Assistant coach Anthony Solomon did a great job tracking Tom Knight. He was a big guy, very skilled, and we knew we were losing ground on Ryan Kelly, who ended up at Duke. So in late September, we went up to watch Tom work out. Rutgers and a few others were there, too. His AAU guy was going to work him out at the high school. For about 10 minutes, he was very impressive. He could run. He had some bounce. He could shoot it. He was skilled. But he looked about 30 pounds overweight and just wasn't in any kind of shape to go for very long. Anthony and I sat there watching him, and we thought: *There's a lot to work with here. We've got to get him in shape. We probably should redshirt him. He's a great student. Let's offer him.*

So we took him and redshirted him. We got him with a nutritionist. Our strength and conditioning coach, Tony Rolinski, broke him down and got him in great shape. He was a little injury-prone early. But like a lot of our guys, he gave us really good minutes as an older player. He really helped us. On the road against South Florida in 2012–13 when we were 3–3 and kind of at a crossroads, he came off the bench and scored 17 points and played great. We won by eight down there and got on a little run and got an NCAA Tournament bid.

I loved his personality. He had an unbelievable sense of humor; he was a little bit of the class clown in the locker room.

The guys were always amazed at how he dressed, his lifestyle, and his responses. He was one of those guys you always like being around.

GARRICK SHERMAN

Associate head coach Rod Balanis and I recruited Garrick Sherman hard in high school before he went to Michigan State. When we heard about his plans to transfer, we felt we'd have a great shot.

What I loved about him was he was a really skilled big guy. With his right or left hand, he could put it on the floor a little bit. He really gave us some good stuff and had a really good sense of humor. There was a tough stretch when he was really not playing much for us as a junior. He didn't play in regulation against Louisville, but he came off the bench, played 22 minutes in the five overtimes, and scored 17 points. The Louisville front line was exhausted, and he kind of won the game for us. All of a sudden, this fresh guy came in and lit it up. I remember Dick Vitale just hammering me, going, "Why doesn't this guy play?"

ZACH AUGUSTE

I didn't feel we had a shot with Zach Auguste, but assistant coach Anthony Solomon kept us in the game. Zach was looking at Florida, Marquette, Providence, and UConn. They all were working him really hard. We were not even being mentioned, but Anthony stayed in touch with his high school coach, and his mom, Leah, understood us. Florida started to fade, and he planned a visit to Notre Dame.

He came in on a Friday, and we had dinner at Ruth's Chris Steak House. I was there early, and Anthony texted me. He was bringing Zach and his mother. Anthony told me, "FYI, he's committing to you when he walks into dinner tonight." We sat down, we had a great dinner, and it was all done.

But we were also recruiting Tyler Cavanaugh, who was visiting Wake Forest, and only had room for one of the two players. We had our own rule. When a kid's making a visit to another school, don't communicate with him. But I said, "Slo, you've got to let Wake Forest know and Cavanaugh know that Zach took the scholarship." Cavanaugh ended up at my alma mater, George Washington, and is now with the Atlanta Hawks.

During Zach's first two years, there were times where I wasn't sure he was going to make it. Then as a junior and senior, he was just fabulous. He made himself into an NBA prospect and now he's in the midst of a great European career. I loved his smile and his upbeat attitude. He was really pure. And I think he benefited from being in our system. It just took two years to grow him.

Demetrius Jackson

Demetrius Jackson was one of those guys you had to get. When you've got a guy like that in your hometown, you have to sign him if your program is going to have any credibility. So I felt an unbelievable amount of pressure to get this one done.

His recruiting was a little bit all over the place. Illinois, Kansas, and Florida State all were in the mix. Through his recruitment I felt like four or five times we were going to get a commitment, and then we didn't. We were in the dance again, and I was a little bit worried about Illinois because they really made a run at him.

The one thing that I thought we always benefited from was that Jackson had never been out of this town much. He had not been on an airplane until he flew to the NBA Players Camp the summer before his senior year of high school. He was a Mishawaka, Indiana, guy and had his friends, his family, and his crew here. And at the end of the day, he wanted to stay close to home. He wanted to be here. Anthony Solomon had done a great job recruiting him since he was in ninth grade. We knew him, and he knew our program and he was over here a lot. So I just felt it was a real feather in our cap to keep a McDonald's All-American in South Bend.

Freshman year was hard for Demetrius. It was new and it was at a whole different level. I suspended him for a week because of his academic habits. During that week he couldn't do anything with the team, but I would bring him in at night and work him out. I'd meet him at 9:00 PM in the Pit. We didn't do much working out, though. We did a lot of talking. I just wanted him to know that I had his back, but there were certain standards he had to hit. And he responded.

He didn't have the freshman year he would have liked. But, man, that next year he was really ready to help us win an ACC championship. There wasn't as much pressure on him because we had Jerian Grant, Pat Connaughton, Zach Auguste, and Steve Vasturia.

He willingly became a great on-ball defender on that team. He could really guard. And we had just a magical run, and he had a great year. He contemplated a little bit about entering the pros, but finally he ended up coming back. My biggest question was if he and Auguste could lead our returning group because we had just lost unbelievable leadership in Connaughton and Grant.

But he really became a leader his junior year, and I'll always be really proud of that. We got back to the Elite Eight, and he kind of drove us there with big plays. He was just fabulous. His last college game was against North Carolina in the NCAA East Regional, and that may have been his best game. He had a game-high 26 points. But then it was time for him to give the pros a try.

He still follows us. I get texts after games. He loved his teammates and misses this culture. That's why I think he watches us so much and tweets about wins or guys having good games.

STEVE VASTURIA

As far as feel for the game on both ends of the floor, Steve Vasturia is maybe the best all-around guy I've ever coached. He had the maturity of a fifth-year senior as an 18-year-old freshman. He was steady emotionally and the same every day. I don't think he missed a practice or a game. It was hard to take him out because we flowed better on both ends of the floor when he was in the game. He made big shots, a lot of really big shots. He made big defensive plays. We had him guard the toughest guy. We even had him guard power forwards sometimes when we downshifted our lineup.

I would tell recruits who were in my office to just watch Vasturia. Watch how he moves without the ball, how he knows when to screen, how he knows when to cut, how he gets to his shot, or how he helps his teammates. He was an unbelievable help defender. He would rotate over and cover up mistakes with charges and rotation. I was calmer when he was in the game because he was just so steady. And he had just an amazing career for us.

The only time I ever saw him show emotion was when he hit that trail three against Kentucky in the NCAA Elite Eight in 2016. Kentucky called timeout, and we led by six with about six minutes to go, and he came to the bench and pumped his fists. And I remember thinking, *Oh, my God, he's never done stuff like that. He's really excited.* The moment was so big and so awesome even he got caught up in it.

Arguably, a shot that would rival Dwight Clay's against UCLA in 1974 was his three in front of our bench in the 2015

ACC Championship game against North Carolina to give us the lead. We kept reversing the ball, Demetrius Jackson made the extra pass, Vasturia banged a three, and we took the lead. It's one of our all-time great shots in program history. He had another one to help us beat Duke as a freshman and one as a senior against Clemson. He had as many big shots at key times as anybody in the history of our program.

He's playing in Germany. He broke his foot in 2017–18. It was the same injury Bonzie Colson had. I had him come out to campus when he was injured because he was getting bored. I said, "I want you to come out because I value your IQ. Would you watch our team and give me feedback?"

He was back here for about a week, and I sat with him at times during practice, asking him, "Well, what do you see? What do you think?" I just so valued his eyes, and it was really helpful.

One time I brought up being a coach. He said, "No, I'm not doing that, Coach." So I think he'll play for a while and then maybe go work on Wall Street.

V.J. BEACHEM

V.J. Beachem was key for us because he was an in-state kid, and that's always important. It was between us and Purdue for him. Assistant coach Anthony Solomon saw him and did a fabulous job from his 10th grade year on, working him, getting him up here in the summer. Beachem came up more unofficially than any kid we ever recruited, and he and his family knew our program well.

He had to get stronger and he did. He came off the bench for us as a young guy and could score it. Then, like a fine wine, he got better with age. We got to those junior and senior years, and he was on the all-NCAA East Regional team. He played great against Michigan in that first-round game in 2016 and had a really good senior year for us. Like many of the guys I've had, when they get to be juniors and seniors, I love the relationships we can have. I can be closer with them and joke with them, but they know when it's time to get down to business—even if I challenge them. That's what I love about this program. It never damages the teacher-pupil relationship. They never take advantage of it. That's never a thought. And that's what I've loved about coaching here and the type of kids we get.

His calm demeanor, along with Steve Vasturia's, was really good for that team. Zach Auguste and Demetrius Jackson were more high-strung guys, so V.J. kept our squad balanced. He made himself an NBA prospect. He was on a two-way deal with the Los Angeles Lakers and just kind of scratching and clawing in the G League, trying to get on a roster. He was just a special kid.

AUSTIN BURGETT

Austin Burgett was an in-state guy who committed early. Anthony Solomon did a great job with him. And we were excited about him because he was a stretch four man with bounce. He had great athletic ability—kind of sneaky athletic ability—but he could just never stay healthy. I felt for him because he just kept getting banged up. One key time was when he was coming off a good game at Florida State, and we were going to start him against North Carolina. Friday practice came, and he sprained his ankle and was out for three weeks. That stuff always seemed to happen.

He had an early heart condition, which was a little scary. We had to work through that. But he was the ultimate team guy, a believer. His attitude was great, even though I know he was very disappointed his career didn't really go how he wanted it to go. He really was a good leader for us as a senior, even though he wasn't playing much with that group. He was just one of those

Even though Mike Krzyzewski and I regularly battle as ACC foes, we remain close, and there's a lot of mutual respect there. (*USA TODAY* Sports Images)

Jerian Grant had a great game to help us upend Duke, the eventual national champion, in 2015. (*USA TODAY* Sports Images)

I pose alongside AP Player of the Year Jimmer Fredette. After we went 27–7 and 14–4 in the Big East in 2011, I was named AP Coach of the Year. (AP Images)

We celebrate our 2015 ACC Tournament title, a sign we really had become a league power. (AP Images)

For a kid who was raised in the Beltway, beating Duke and North Carolina en route to winning the 2015 ACC Tournament was just special. (AP Images)

Pat Connaughton goes to the basket against undefeated Kentucky during the Elite Eight in 2015. Referees who officiated that game still tell me it was one of the best they've ever seen. (*USA TODAY* Sports Images)

Demetrius Jackson, who had two steals in the last 30 seconds of the game, helps push us past Wisconsin with this layup and into the Elite Eight in 2016. (AP Images)

Our student section has really become a great thing and a real home-court advantage at Notre Dame. (*USA TODAY* Sports Images)

I loved coaching Matt Farrell, who was recommended to me by another point guard I coached, Bobby Hurley. (*USA TODAY* Sports Images)

I get ready for the 2017 Maui Invitational, which was an incredible experience. Our team played with such great energy. (*USA TODAY* Sports Images)

I had good reason to celebrate after we came back against Wichita State to win the 2017 Maui Invitational. (*USA TODAY* Sports Images)

I address our home crowd after passing the great Digger Phelps as the all-time winningest basketball coach at Notre Dame. (Lighthouse Imaging)

I love working in the Notre Dame basketball offices, and my goal always has been to retire here. (Lighthouse Imaging)

I'm so proud of our 2018 senior class. They not only won a ton of big games, but they also were great kids off the court. (Lighthouse Imaging)

When the 2018 class graduated, it was a special moment for me. They represent the university so well. (Alan Wasielewski)

guys where injuries never let him get on any consistent track. Burgett stays in touch with us. He's playing in Europe now, and I miss his sense of humor and personality.

BONZIE COLSON

We were out at the Nike EYBL event in Anaheim, California, in April of Bonzie Colson's junior year in high school. I was watching a game, and assistant coach Martin Ingelsby was sitting with me. Ingelsby left to go watch another game on another court and he said, "Hey, Coach, while you're sitting here, see the kid playing on the next court down with BABC [Boston Amateur Basketball Club]? Just watch him. He's intriguing. He just gets stuff done. I don't know what position he plays, but he just is efficient."

So I watched him, and he gets a tip-in. I watched him a little more, and he hit a 15-footer. Then he got an offensive rebound against some big guys. This is all the type of stuff he ended up doing for us. We went to dinner that night, and I said, "Martin, you're right. He is intriguing. Make sure I watch him twice tomorrow."

I watched two of his games on that last day and liked him even more. And we have had a lot of guys who didn't have a position. We've built a program like that. What position was Luke Harangody? What was Pat Connaughton? We get basketball players and we figure it out.

I like Colson's bloodlines. His dad, Bonzie Sr., a former Rhode Island player, was a D.C. guy from Dunbar High School, so he and I still have DeMatha-Dunbar arguments. His dad was on Al Skinner's staff at Boston College, so Bonzie had been around the gym his whole life. Ed Cooley coached with his father at Boston College and is godfather to Bonzie's sister. So when Cooley took over as Providence head coach, that looked like a potential destination for Bonzie. But by the end of the summer, it came down to Notre Dame and Florida State.

A longtime AAU guy and Boston Celtics scout, Leo Papile, runs BABC. He's been around a while. He's watched our program and he was talking to us, saying, "He's your kind of guy." And he was right. He was selling it as a great fit, and we agreed.

I remember Bonzie's dad saying to me, "Coach, I was taught to hate you guys at Boston College, but I'm coming around. Just work with me here."

You could see Bonzie as a face-up four, a little like Connaughton. He played away from the bucket a lot in high school. He would make plays and he would drive it. The Nike Elite Youth Basketball League has most of the best players. They do six or seven tournaments through the spring and summer. In their analytics Bonzie was the No. 2 guy in overall efficiency, and he was playing against all the guys he would play against at Notre Dame. He had to play with a chip on his shoulder against bigger dudes, future lottery picks, guys that people just thought were better than him. His approach was: "Who's coming at me today? I'm a junk-yard dog. I'm gonna do it."

It took me a while to put him in a game, but we charted his first 25 practices into the preseason of his freshman year, and he was the second leading rebounder in practice behind Zach Auguste. He was right there on all the efficiency stuff just like he was in the EYBL. He was battling in the paint, getting his hands on balls, and making plays.

There's no question that playing five out and playing smaller helped him because he had all that room in the lane and down low. The spacing was really good that way, and he was handling the ball every two or three passes. He energized everybody. He was a big-moment guy.

He was yet another example of our theme of guys getting better here. Guys improve here. Bonzie struggled a bit as a freshman. But a game at Georgia Tech was his coming-out party, and after that, he added something every year to his game. He added passing as a sophomore. All of a sudden, his court vision was better, and he was finding our shooters. And then his junior year, he stretched the floor and improved his shooting. The three-point shot became part of his arsenal.

And then as a senior, we moved him all over the court. Until he got hurt, we used his versatility. It's sad; he was in the midst of another fabulous year, a National Player of the Year kind of season. I don't know if I've ever been more heartbroken about an injury than I was with him. His senior year would have been a great story. College basketball missed him. People loved to talk about him. The media loved him. Coaches loved him. I got a ton of texts from other coaches when we announced his injury.

Usually when great players are hurt, they kind of get in their own world, trying to get rehabbed and thinking about their professional futures and how they're going to get healthy. That's not necessarily a bad thing, but Bonzie never showed any of that. He was supportive of his teammates. He was helping them on the bench, he was helping them in the locker room, he was constantly talking about coming back.

I wanted to be very smart with this young man because of all he gave our program. The Colson family felt it was absolutely handled the way it should have been handled. That was their theme all along. In the back of my mind, I was thinking, *Maybe I shouldn't bring him back.* But Bonzie wanted to play. He was in the training room constantly, doing whatever he needed to do. There was a lot of discussion, and everybody was in the loop. If Bonzie had ever said, "I don't want to come back," we would have respected that. I told Bonzie and his parents that he wasn't going to be letting anyone down if he decided against playing that last year. I put that out there the week after his surgery. But he did come back, and I've never been prouder of a guy.

AUSTIN TORRES

When Austin Torres committed, I think there was a line in the *South Bend Tribune* that said Notre Dame hadn't recruited a kid from the area in 30 years and that we took two in a week. Torres was our Granger, Indiana, guy.

I knew his mother, Brenda, because she worked on my Coaches vs. Cancer program as a volunteer. She always was part of the Night of the Stars event in August. He and Demetrius Jackson were on the same AAU team. So when we were recruiting Jackson, that whole summer all I did was watch that team play, and so I saw Torres play a lot.

Brenda came to me in August and said, "What do you think about Austin's recruiting?" I offered her a few thoughts on some of the schools they had been considering. And she asked, "Is it all right if I call you just for some advice on who's recruiting him?" I, of course, said sure, but I never thought we were going to offer him.

But when we were going through our depth chart and our board while waiting on Jackson, the question became: who else are we going to add to our class? We were looking for athletic ability, somebody with some bounce. I said, "You know what? I saw Torres play 20 times. The guy flies around. He may not score a lot for us, but he just flies all over the place."

We kept talking about him, but we didn't do anything about it. Then he committed to Central Michigan. And it's the only time I've done this with a guy. I've not really recruited committed guys.

But he was a local kid. His mom went to Notre Dame, and his father, Oscar McBride, played football at Notre Dame. They were such a Notre Dame family. I talked to my staff and finally I said, "Well, I'm going to make an executive decision here. I'm going to call and offer him. He may tell me, 'Hey, Coach, I'm committed,' but I'm going to offer him."

We did that, and he said, "Well, Coach, I'd really like to talk about that. That was always a dream for me."

I said, "Well, no pressure. Let me come out to the house this week and let's talk about it."

After he had been committed for two or three weeks, Anthony Solomon and I got in the car and did a home visit right here in town. Now I know how guys who recruit in Philly and New York do it; they just drive around from one neighborhood to the next. Slo and I were driving, and I said, "Can you believe we're doing a home visit in our own neighborhood, in Granger, where we live?"

Torres took our offer, and we talked about redshirting him, but he and Jackson were excited about coming in together. Torres was that athletic guy, that versatile guy who could just fly around. It took him a little while to get in better shape, and various injuries set him back. He, though, helped us win a lot of games through doing a lot of the dirty work

His final year came during our injury-plagued season in 2017–18, and as the fifth-year guy, his leadership and some of the things he said in the locker room were very powerful. I was really proud of the tone he set. He ended up in a starting role for a while because of his toughness and his activity. He just flew around and gave us stuff.

He wants to be a coach, and he and I have talked about it. He's a Michiana guy, and I don't know if he's going anywhere else.

MARTINAS GEBEN

Eric Atkins' coach was Pat Clatchey, the coach at Mount Saint Joe in the Catholic League in Baltimore whom I have the utmost respect for. Clatchey called me when Martinas Geben was in 10th grade. They had played against him, and he said, "Hey, there's a kid here you've got to watch, a Lithuanian kid."

So we got him on the radar, and associate head coach Rod Balanis did a great job tracking him. He played on that same AAU team with Jerian Grant and D.J. Harvey and played at a high level in the Nike EYBL circuit. I loved him as soon as I got to see him on that circuit. We offered him quickly in the spring of his junior year and recruited him hard through the summer. It came down to Notre Dame and Virginia.

He was not Catholic, but his being in a Catholic high school helped us connect with him more here, and he later converted to Catholicism. I was really proud of the man he became. He was not the most confident player as a young guy. He doubted himself sometimes, but we got him in better shape.

After his sophomore year, he was really thinking about transferring because we had Zach Auguste and Bonzie Colson playing inside. The day after we got back from Philadelphia after losing in the 2016 Elite Eight to North Carolina, I said to him, "Come by my office." He was the only guy I was going to meet with that week. I told the rest of them, "I'm going to give you guys some time to get rested and get back in gear academically."

I said, "Martin, you're the only guy I brought in—because I know where your head's at. You're concerned about your future here and you may not have a decision on it today, but here's what I want you to think about as you're contemplating if you're going to stay or you're going to go: you're starting next year. When practice starts in June, you're going to be in a white shirt all summer. You better never come into the gym in a blue shirt. That's my plan for you moving forward. So digest that, think about that. If you need a release and you need to go look at schools, I'll fully support you on that. Why don't you think about it for a week and come back next week?"

I think Geben loved Notre Dame. He loved the academic setting he was in, loved the Catholicism, loved his teammates. He came back the next week and said, "Well, Coach, I appreciate that. You're right. I've got to get in better shape and I've got to be better for you."

I said, "Well, I'm going to help you on that. But you're our starting guy. You're starting."

He started early his junior year, and then we changed the lineup after the North Carolina game and we downshifted and played small. V.J. Beachem was the four, so now he was out of the loop again. But at the end of that year, he came back off the bench and gave us good minutes. He was trending toward a big senior year, and we needed him to have a great one for us.

What got him over the hump was being the starting center on Lithuania's national team. That squad beat Purdue, and he came back with a gold medal. He showed it off for two weeks, carried it around everywhere, which was just awesome. His teammates were giving him a hard time, joking, "Can you put that thing away?"

He started his senior season unbelievably confident for us. He and Colson, two senior big guys, they'd been through it all and they were playing well off of each other. Then in the title game in Maui, Geben was at the line, and his two free throws would make or break that game. As he was going to the line, I was just saying to myself, *Never has a young man deserved for these two to go down. He's a good kid, he's a believer, he wants to do well.*

Of course, the first one hung on the rim there for a little bit. Maybe there was some divine intervention, and the lady on the dome blew it in. They both ended up going in, and we won.

After that he was really confident. When the word came that Bonzie was out, we had a meeting with the whole team. I said, "Well, what are your guys' thoughts? Everybody tell me."

They were going down the line, and Geben was about the third or fourth guy. He said, "Everybody's got to do more, Coach. Everybody's got to do more."

I said, "That's a great way of putting it."

And he was unbelievable. He became a double-double guy, one of four in the ACC. He led, he took on front lines, and he was just physical. And I was so happy for him. He certainly helped his professional stock and made himself an NBA prospect.

Matt Farrell

When Demetrius Jackson was a freshman and was suspended for a week, one thing I brought up in a meeting was that maybe we needed an insurance policy at point guard if Jackson couldn't get it in gear. After all, we didn't have another point guard. So assistant coach Martin Ingelsby did a great job tracking this kid who had just de-committed from Boston College. It was Matt Farrell. We had people in New Jersey say: "Tough guy, tough son of a gun, edgy, Bobby Hurley-like." All that came from basketball people you respected. So I went to see him.

I flew into Newark and I was in the Newark Airport Marriott. I was walking through the lobby to my rental car to drive down to Point Pleasant Beach on the shore to watch his game. I got a call, and it was a 201 area code, which is North Jersey. I heard, "Coach, it's Bob Hurley." I thought it was Bob Hurley Sr., but it was Bobby, even though he didn't say it was Bobby Hurley.

The then-coach of Buffalo said, "Hey, I just wanted to check in. I don't usually do this, but I want to let you know that I've seen Matt Farrell, and he can really play."

Meanwhile, I'm completely confused, and then finally he said something that clicked, and I said, "Okay, Bobby, this is you. I keep thinking it's your dad."

He said, "No, Coach, this is Bobby. I was trying like heck to get Matt Farrell at Buffalo. I know I couldn't get him, Coach. And since I can't get him, I want to really recommend him." And then next came the best line. He said, "Coach, he really reminds me of me."

I said, "Well, I should just offer him right now. This is over. That's the best endorsement I could ever get."

Now I'm really excited. I've got about a two-hour drive down to the Jersey shore and I can't wait to get there and see this kid. And he didn't disappoint. He zipped through stuff, making shots and throwing passes all over. So I offered him that night. I made sure he knew before I left the gym.

I came to find out his grandfather went to Notre Dame, so there was this dream school that was now talking to him. Two days later he committed. He hadn't even made a visit yet. I said, "We'll bring you out in the spring."

He actually committed while we were at the 2014 ACC Tournament, the day before we lost to Wake Forest in the first round. It ended ugly for us in the play-in game, but if there was one positive that week, it's that Farrell committed. I was hanging on that.

The next year he was a freshman on the ACC championship team. And we had Jerian Grant and Jackson, so he was playing against NBA-caliber guards every day. We ran game situations a lot in practice and we had to stop doing them because he was on the blue team. The white team could never win a game situation, and I was worried about their psyche—that they'd think they couldn't win a close game. And it's because Farrell was in there throwing in a three, throwing in a runner, making a pass, just doing his typical I-95 Jersey stuff. I call it the "I-95 edge." There's just some I-95 edge with guys from out east. We just felt really, really good about him. But we couldn't get him in the game because we had all those other guys.

The next year he was a sophomore, and we still had Jackson, Steve Vasturia, and V.J. Beachem, so the perimeter was pretty solid. Matt was not really playing much, and probably the dagger for him was when we went to Syracuse, and Jackson was hurt. I played Vasturia at the point. That was a big mistake on my part. We should have had him more ready to play, but I thought Vasturia would handle the point, and then we lost.

Matt came into my office a couple times to see me. He never complained, just wanted to know if there was a plan for him. With about a month left in that season, I said, "Matt, I know right now it doesn't look good and I understand you may need to go somewhere to play. I get all that. And if that's the case, I'll help you with that. But can you hang in there? I've seen crazier stuff that has happened. Just hang in there with us. Who knows how this thing is going to end?"

We used him late to help us get the ball up court quicker and to take some of the ballhandling off Jackson's plate. His first start was an NCAA Tournament game against Michigan. And he played fabulously. He had five points, four assists. The next night against Stephen F. Austin, we really needed another ballhandler because of all the pressure they put on us. He was driving, he was playing great. Against Wisconsin we threw him to the wolves, and he delivered. So not only did he help us advance to another NCAA Elite Eight, it saved him from transferring. I dodged a bullet. Now I was saying, "It's your ball. You're the guy." The transfer stuff was not even a discussion anymore.

Then as a junior, he had a great year for us. The coming-out party was the Legends Classic where he was the MVP back in Brooklyn again. He was being talked about as the most improved player in the country; he had come completely out of nowhere. He got us back to the NCAA Tournament, just a great story.

He went into his senior year as one of the better point guards in the country. I went to ACC Media Day with Bonzie Colson and Farrell—two rocks, two guys who were great examples of our program, two seniors who had won together. And because of those guys, we were picked third in the preseason poll, and there were great expectations. And rightfully so. Then it was frustrating to not see those guys be able to do their thing because they were primed to lead their team. We saw a glimpse of it in Maui. But after both Farrell and Colson went down with injuries, Maui seemed like ancient history.

Eric Katenda

Eric Katenda went from Cheshire Academy in Connecticut to Sunrise Christian Academy in Kansas. We had recruited him at Cheshire, and when he transferred, we followed him. He ended up being a spring signee. After our season was over, I went over to watch a workout, and an Oklahoma assistant was there with me. They played pickup, and the Oklahoma coach turned to me and said, "I think he's a pro. He reminds me of Luol Deng."

I'm looking at him and said, "I don't disagree with you."

So I got back on the plane and called Martin Ingelsby, who did a lot of the work on him. I said, "God, he was good. We've got to really try to get him."

It came down to us and Wake Forest, and we ended up getting him. Then he was unable to attend summer school because the NCAA would not certify one of his English courses. So he went to play a three-on-three pickup game at a playground in D.C., just to get a workout in. A freak accident occurred; a guy swiped at the ball with his hand and—while doing so—detached Katenda's retina. Eric was so quiet, and by the time they realized it wasn't just a scratch, it ruptured, and he lost the sight in his right eye.

We wanted him to know he had a full scholarship at Notre Dame, no matter what happened. He had surgery and he came to us in August. I got a call from Jon Scheyer, who played at Duke and is now on the staff there, because he had the same situation. He called and asked if he could talk to Eric, and Scheyer turned out to be a good resource for him. There were some other stories of that happening to players; Amar'e Stoudemire was another, and we were able to give those to Katenda.

What I loved about him was he never felt sorry for himself. He was always like, "Coach, I'm going to be fine." Each week during his freshman year he'd get a little better and adjust. Sometimes there were areas where he couldn't see an open player, but as his eye doctor said, it's amazing how the one eye takes over and the body just adjusts as far as depth perception and everything else.

He became really a heck of a practice player for us. The problem was he had other health issues, and he never was able to stay healthy enough to play. But he was very good in practice, was a great team guy. He graduated, he's playing in England now, and doing well.

But it was sad because I always think back to that workout at Sunrise Academy with the assistant from Oklahoma. I walked away saying, "He's better than what I saw earlier in the fall; he's passing and making shots."

I think he really appreciated his time here. Everybody was so very supportive of him. During the games he did play in, our bench couldn't have been happier for him.

REX PFLUEGER

Rex Pflueger was one of those kids we weren't doing much with because I was never really confident recruiting out West; I'm still not. I don't want to waste time in California. At the end of the day, most of the kids that we want to get out of there are going to stay in the Pac-12.

During the summer before Pflueger's senior year, I was at the Adidas event in Vegas. Martin Ingelsby had recruited him, and Pflueger's coach, Mater Dei High's Gary McKnight, was a big supporter of our program. Gary and I have been close for some time. I was walking to the restroom, and Pflueger's parents, who I didn't know at the time, continued to make eye contact and kind of acknowledge me. We weren't permitted to talk, but they made things quite obvious. I said to Martin, "The couple sitting behind the bench right there, who are they?"

He said, "Those are Rex Pflueger's parents."

I said, "I've been doing this a long time, Martin. I think I can read acknowledgments and body language. They keep getting my attention and waving. Let's follow up. What's going on with his recruiting?"

Martin said Stanford was involved, but the Cardinal had just received a commitment from a guard in Atlanta. So Stanford was off the board. Pflueger was not really looking at anybody else in the Pac-12—maybe Washington State a little bit, maybe Texas A&M because his dad went there. I said to Martin, "Have you watched him much?"

He said, "Coach, he can really guard. He's athletic. He's a tough kid."

We were going to the Peach Jam the next week, so I said, "Make sure I watch him and let's make the call."

The family said they'd be really interested, but I was still wondering if he'd leave the West Coast. Rex was really good on the phone, a sharp kid even as a young guy. He said, "Coach, I'm not locked into staying out here. I may want to get out of here and do something different. I've been in California my whole life."

I watched him play one game down at the Peach Jam. And he was typical Pflueger, flying around everywhere. He was playing for the Oakland Soldiers down there. We got the word back to McKnight. I said, "I just want you to know we're offering him tonight. We love him, we want him. Tell me what I need to do. I want a Mater Dei guy."

So now we were recruiting him hard, and it got interesting. We had Pflueger and Jalen Coleman, who we were recruiting out of Indianapolis. We brought them both in for the first home football weekend. We were trying to pull it off where we could take them both because we had room. But as we got into it, it looked like we probably couldn't get both. We were going to have to get one or the other. They both left campus, and I actually went to Coleman's house on a Tuesday in Indianapolis. He had the first shot, and if he had taken it, Pflueger probably wouldn't have ended up coming to Notre Dame. Then I was going to Los Angeles the next day to meet Martin, and we were going to sit with the Pfluegers.

Coleman said he wanted to take a visit to UNLV. So obviously they were not ready. I had a nice dinner with them and I got the vibe. I went back to the hotel, flew to John Wayne Airport the next day, and Martin picked me up. We went to Mater Dei to watch the workout, and Gary had all kinds of prospects—so there were maybe eight coaches in his office. He said, "Mike, come back here." We went back in the equipment room and had some privacy. He said, "Look, I don't know anything about the Coleman kid you're recruiting. But just from talking to the Pflueger family, I don't think they'd be comfortable if you get Coleman."

We went to dinner that night at the Pfluegers' home in Dana Point. At the end of the evening, I said, "Hey, I just want to be clear. It's yours to take. I think Jalen Coleman's going to make another visit, but he could call me tomorrow and say he's coming. And we can only take one of you."

So we shook hands and left the house. We were 10 minutes from the house, and Rex called me and said, "Coach, I want you to know I'm coming to Notre Dame."

Rex was turning the ball over that summer before his freshman year in practices and he was so hard on himself. He's just so intense. He would get really emotional sometimes when he didn't play well. As we were really getting to know his psyche, it was about how to loosen him up and get him to relax. He was not playing much his freshman year and he was struggling with that. But we came out of that and we started to think we had to have a guy who guards and does the dirty work.

When we won against Duke in Cameron while he was a freshman, he played really well. He made a big three at the end of the shot clock and got a key rebound because of his nose for the ball. And, of course, he was a key guy through the NCAA

Tournament and made the tip-in against Stephen F. Austin to get us to the Sweet 16. He also made the key steal and got the key rebound. He made another game-sealing tip-in against Syracuse in 2018. He's just a winner.

He's a neat kid to coach because there's a maturity about him where you can mess with him, talk to him, and have fun with him. Then when it's time to get to work, he's really intense. He is a gem to coach, he's got an edge about him, and he's a tough dude. He's improved his offensive game and has become a leader for us now.

T.J. Gibbs

I always felt we would have a shot with T.J. Gibbs because his dad reached out to assistant coach Anthony Solomon about Ashton Gibbs, T.J.'s older brother, who ended up at Pittsburgh. So I knew they respected our program. We had too many guards at the time; so we never recruited Ashton, who ended up having a great career at Pitt. But we invested in T.J. early. We were really watching him all of his junior year. We were at the school a lot.

We got him in for an official visit and we felt we were in great shape. He was down to Georgetown, Notre Dame, and Oklahoma. This was the third kid of the family who had gone through the recruiting deal, so they understood how it worked. While T.J. Gibbs was on his visit Notre Dame, his parents were a little distracted because Sterling Gibbs was in the process of transferring from Seton Hall to UConn but was still getting recruiting calls. So T.J. said to his parents, "You do that. I got this." Unbeknownst to them, he committed at breakfast with us before he left. The parents had no idea.

To see his improvement from freshman year to sophomore year was just amazing. He's also a fearless guy. You could tell he was the youngest of three and had to fight for his life in the gym when dad worked him out. I love his personality. He's got that smile that lights up a room. There's always good energy coming off of him. He takes losing so hard. He's very hard on himself. Like with Rex Pflueger, I've tried to work to get him to not be as hard on himself after he makes a mistake or has a bad game.

JOHN MOONEY

I was at my beach house in Rehoboth Beach, Delaware, in August before John Mooney's senior year. A call came in, and it was Billy Donovan. He had taken the Oklahoma City Thunder job back in April so he had only been there a few months. I said, "Billy, how is everything, the transition? Going well?"

He said, "Mike, it's different."

Then he said, "Do you know who Johnny Mooney is?"

I had no idea. Mooney had committed to Florida when he was a young kid so he was off the board. Donovan's son and Mooney played together on the same team. So Donovan saw him when he was 14, loved him, and was able to secure an early commitment to Florida. At the time I was thinking Mooney was a graduate assistant that Billy was recommending. Billy said, "Well, I don't really want to be in the middle of this nor should I, but the dad called me. Johnny committed to us in 10th grade. He's 6'9", a stretch four, and, Mike, I think he's a hell of a prospect. He was all set to go to Florida all the way up until they had their Elite camp in early August. I don't know how much they really want Johnny. And the dad called me and said they'd really be interested in Notre Dame and asked if I knew Mike Brey. Mike, he would be great for you."

I got off the phone with Donovan and called Mooney's father. I said, "We'd love you to visit Labor Day weekend, three weeks away."

We recruited him for just those few weeks. He made the visit and committed to us. He also visited Wake Forest, Alabama, Georgia, pretty much the whole SEC. They were all finding out who he was. He's a Catholic kid, and his style of play obviously was great for us. The night Mooney hit the six three-pointers in Chapel Hill against North Carolina in 2018, I was thinking Donovan probably had Big Monday, ESPN's big basketball showcase, on and thought he found the right place for his guy. I teased him over the phone and said, "You are my new recruiting coordinator. Got anybody else for me? Call me with anybody else."

Elijah Burns

He came from a really good program at Blair Academy. There's a scouting service guy in New Jersey, Ed Butler, who is very well respected and has been doing it for a long time. He called us when Elijah Burns was in 10th grade and he knew our program and our profile. He said, "This kid, Elijah Burns, would be a good fit for you guys."

Elijah was injury-prone a little bit. He was in and out playing. And when he played for the Albany City Rocks, they didn't make the A Circuit or qualify for the Peach Jam. They were playing off-site at the B level, and we were following him there. He was a kid who certainly knew our academics and knew our program. And like Carleton Scott, he committed without seeing the school. The biggest thing was getting him healthy. He was out with an ankle injury most of his senior year of high school, and we redshirted him to help him get back.

He got himself in shape, grew out of the injury stuff, and became a good front-line guy for us. He's one of those who has really gotten everything out of the university; he's maxed out his Notre Dame experience. He went to Africa to study and took another internship. He's a really cool kid and absolutely taking advantage of the Notre Dame thing as an undergrad.

MATT GREGORY

Even as a freshman, Matt Gregory was maybe one of the most mature guys we've ever had. He was like a rock. The players loved him. I was so happy that we were able to give him a scholarship for 2017–18. He deserved it. He really had a finger on the pulse of our team. Because he had great insight to our team, I'd sometimes ask him, "What do you think? What do you see? How's our group?"

D.J. HARVEY

We went back to the DeMatha well to get D.J. Harvey and were on him for a while. And I think one of the main reasons we got him was we hung in there with him. A bunch of people offered him, and then he cooled off a little bit. Maybe people thought DeMatha didn't win enough games while he was there, but we liked his body type and skillset. We felt we could coach and develop him. I think he visited Alabama, but it was really us at the end of the day. Maryland and Villanova both wavered on him.

With the whole DeMatha thing and my connection there and Jerian Grant's success, my recruiting pitch was: "I'm going to take care of DeMatha guys. I have to. There's pressure for me. You have to make it, or I can never go back to my alma mater."

So I think he really found that we had his back. It was an interesting dynamic for him because he was the only freshman his first year, and that's a little different. You don't have another guy there with you and you're with an older team. I give our older players credit. They took him under their wing. The biggest thing he learned was how to be a good teammate. He was a little bit of a loner, not much of a vocal guy. I said to him, "You play the game by yourself sometimes. You don't engage your teammates much. One of the biggest things you may get out of this year is you're learning to be a better teammate and interacting with your teammates because you have unbelievable examples."

In our culture I really saw him grow in that sense. I'd see him and Nik Djogo working out at night. And he used to be a lone wolf. I felt for him because if he wasn't injured in 2017–18, I think he would have had a John Mooney type of impact for us.

NIKOLA DJOGO

We found Nikola Djogo while we were recruiting Thon Maker, the big kid now with the Milwaukee Bucks. I coached Maker's guardian at the Metropolitan Area Basketball School when he was a young guy. And so we thought if he went to college maybe we could get him. To this day, Maker says he would have come to Notre Dame if he had gone to college.

Assistant coach Anthony Solomon and I were going up there once a week in September to check out Maker. By the second time, we were also watching this guard. He was interesting. Big, long, and athletic, he could run and shoot it. The second time I saw him, Djogo got bopped in the head during a scrimmage and was cut a little bit, but he came back out. Maybe the school didn't have a trainer there or something, but to stop the bleeding, he was holding a roll of toilet paper to his head while sitting on the bench. So I went over and sat down with him after practice. I was looking at this kid as he was still bleeding. I said, "Nik, who is recruiting you? Where are you visiting?"

He said, "Penn really wants me, Coach, but the financial package isn't going to work there." He's a great student and he told me he was visiting Northeastern that next weekend.

I said, "Do you know anything about our school?"

And he goes, "Coach, I know you've got the No. 1 business school."

I told him, "It's interesting. We came up to see Thon, and you've really grown on me. Do me a favor. Don't commit to Northeastern this week, and I'll get back to you."

At the time we were involved with Javin DeLaurier from Charlottesville, Virginia, who we felt we had a shot at. But Duke got in on him late, and the chances of us landing him were starting to fade. I went to see DeLaurier on a Monday, and Djogo was back from the Northeastern visit. My vibe on DeLaurier was different. So I walked out and called Slo. I said, "We're not getting him. I'm going to offer Nik."

We got Djogo down the next weekend for a visit, and he committed.

We redshirted him. We felt he was a big, gifted guard and we wanted to get him in our culture and grow him, and he really has made great strides. He's gotten better with the ball, though he can still improve defensively. He's a great kid, who is a team-first guy. Who would have thought that Djogo would be in the starting lineup when we played at Duke, where DeLaurier ended up enrolling, in 2018? You just never know how things will play out.

Coaches vs. Cancer
and the NABC

I GOT STARTED WITH THE COACHES VS. CANCER PROGRAM BECAUSE my dad had a malignant melanoma. I was at Duke at the time and was able to get him down into the Duke Cancer Center. They did a magnificent job. He had to have a lot of surgery, but it was successful. So I had a cancer survivor close to home. That happened in 1994, and in '95 I got the Delaware job. At Delaware we had the "three-point attack" for Coaches vs. Cancer where you bid on how many three-pointers were made by the program. The local American Cancer Society office in Delaware was really supportive.

I have had a lot of teams that can make threes, that can really shoot it, so it was a great way to raise money. And my inspiration was my dad. It was mainly because of him that we were doing it. When I came to Notre Dame, we got it all started, and the community has really embraced it. We have a golf tournament, a Night of the Stars, and other events. It has become this big weekend in August, and we have raised around $3 million in South Bend.

What these initiatives did for me at Delaware was to show me in another light. It helps you in the community—and I tell other coaches to get involved with charities—because it gets you around your season-ticket holders and fans. They get to know you a little bit better. Then when you have those tough years, they have a different perspective on who you really are beyond just the basketball parts of it.

As many questions as I got when I was out in public about how Bonzie Colson or Matt Farrell was doing, I also heard a lot of, "Coach, we really appreciate the Coaches vs. Cancer program. I'm going to be there because my dad just survived prostate cancer." It's amazing the personal stories that come with that. And we've been consistently in the top five among schools in funds raised.

I went over and did a breakfast with our former All-American John Paxson, who is now in the Chicago Bulls' front office, in October 2017 to jumpstart initiatives in Chicago. We raised about $30,000. We had a great Q&A session. It was so good that people wouldn't leave.

Then I jumped into the Men of Heart programs through the American Heart Association. My story is personal. When I was 48, I was having shortness of breath and pain in my arm while I was working out after the season. I thought, *I'm not in this bad of shape.* I immediately got tested, and they put a stent in because one artery was 90 percent blocked.

We started a three-pronged program where we do a tip-off event, and I've seen guys who have come back 25 pounds lighter. We've got a nutritionist and we talk about heart health. Barbecue with Brey is another arm of that fund-raiser. The first year we put people in the program through some drills, and they were really low maintenance. Martin Ingelsby had a group down in the Pit, our practice facility. He said, "Let's just do layup lines at half speed," and one guy takes two steps and blows out his Achilles. I felt awful about that.

At the NCAA Final Four, I'm on the Coaches vs. Cancer council. We meet there annually, and there generally are a lot of heavy hitters from the American Cancer Society there. We talk about new areas and new things that could become part of the program. Scott Thompson, who was one of Digger Phelps' assistant coaches and went on to coach at Iowa, Arizona, Rice, Wichita State, and Cornell, is doing a lot to fight cancer around the country.

I've also been on the board of the National Association of Basketball Coaches (NABC) for almost a decade. I'll be president in 2019–20. It's all for the good of the game and how to improve. I'm very much into how we as coaches can help. I was on the NCAA Men's Basketball Rules Committee awhile back and I was chair of that committee at one point. That's a time-consuming job, but it's an important one for our game.

The NABC also asked me to be on an ad hoc committee to interact with the commission that our president at Notre Dame, Father John Jenkins, is on, so I'm part of that. My thing has always been to be part of this conversation and to give back and to help young coaches. I've had a lot of young coaches who reach out to me at the NCAA Final Four. I was very lucky because I had some guys—like a Lon Kruger, who has been at Kansas State, Illinois, Florida, UNLV, and now Oklahoma—who were good to me when I was a young coach. You could talk to him and ask questions. That's so important to do. As a matter of fact, when North Carolina State played us in 2018, I told Wolfpack coach Kevin Keatts, "You're one of our great young ones. Keep doing your thing."

He said, "Coach, I appreciate that."

It's about empowering the next wave of guys. So I'll go through the NABC presidency and then serve one more year after that. And then you usually rotate off, though they brought some guys back, like Syracuse's Jim Boeheim and Michigan State's Tom Izzo, in an emeritus status. It's been interesting to hear the inner workings behind the scenes, how the NABC interacts with the NCAA and with TV contracts and all of those things. You're trying to improve so many areas.

I was really plugged into this latest national conversation because I sit on the NABC board. We had more conference calls than I want to count to talk about ideas, and those discussions were about being part of the solution. It was exciting for me to be so connected with Father John for six months after he was named to the Rice Commission. We were joined at the hip; we spent a lot of time talking about issues in between his meetings.

After the FBI wiretap scandal, college basketball was at a low point, but I do think this is a good thing because we needed an explosion to start this thing over. We have tried at times to suggest things and we tried at times to have some basketball rules that were more sport-specific. We've been pushing for that for 10 years. Men's college basketball is different, and maybe it was going to take something drastic to change it.

I'm encouraged. I don't think we have all the answers yet, but we are addressing the issues. I think the NBA has been forced into helping us now. The league will be be involved with this thing—in particular, any change to the one-and-done rule. NCAA president Mark Emmert has done a really good job to speed up the legislative cycle. So many items that come from what the commission recommended are going to be pushed through, starting in the fall of 2018.

We needed something to swing this narrative back. When all this broke with the wiretaps and the FBI, college basketball coaches were painted with a broad brush as being part of the problem. Since then, and by way of the NABC being the mouthpiece for our coaching fraternity, the suggestions that we put forth are becoming more of the solution. Almost all of the NABC suggestions came back out of the Rice Commission. They jumped on them, liked them, shaped them a little bit. So we, as coaches, had a big say. They listened to us in terms of trying to help this situation. So, overall, I like where the profession is trending.

We want to get the high school coaches back involved in the recruiting process, and they may be part of two weekends in June to help us evaluate players. Each state may have something different in terms of team camps or jamborees. How do we shape the July recruiting period with some sort of NABC/NBA/USA Basketball-run combines and clinics? That's a lot of work, but it's going to be done. The June/July recruiting calendar for 2019 will look completely different than it does now, and that's a good thing.

The main theme that kept coming back to the Rice Commission was the importance of trying to control some of the third-party influences. One change that helps already is that in the offseason we can work with our players four hours per week (instead of two as the rules allowed previously).

In Condoleezza Rice's world, these recommendations mean "get this stuff done." Some of these policies were enacted over the summer of 2018, and others will take some time, but they will happen. The compliance aspect will take time too. Same with the image and likeness conversation because of the ongoing legal process. Right now Condoleezza is our college basketball czar, and she is getting things done. I'm excited that we've swung back toward coaches being part of the solution.

I'm in agreement with players being able to make some money off their likenesses and I think that is something that is going to be out there. If a Bonzie Colson can make some money off his likenesses, that's fair. I think that should be looked at. So there's going to be some major changes and some good ones coming.

Afterword

WHEN YOU TALK ABOUT MIKE BREY, YOU'RE TALKING ABOUT ONE of the great human beings of all time. He's a great coach, a great teacher, a great person, a great friend. It's almost impossible to totally describe him because he's such a fabulous and unique guy. In watching Mike as a player at DeMatha—and he was one of our good ones—he was a coach on the floor. He understood the game. And what a competitor. He would do anything it took to make every possession the best one of the game, including taking a charge or diving for loose balls. He did it all. He had a great way to distribute the ball. He knew who should be looking for the next shot, who we needed to be set up, and what's the best way to get it done. He just had an incredible feel for the game.

We were very fortunate that he wanted to get into coaching when he finished his college career at George Washington. He started with us at DeMatha. We had a lot of coaches through the years come here. At one time we had 13 head coaches at the Division I level. And yet, among all of them, there was none better than Mike. When Mike was playing at George Washington, we would go down and watch his games. Quite naturally, he finished as a team captain down there, too, as well as one of their really great players. He took great care of their team.

We talked basketball back and forth all the time. Mike had worked at our basketball camp during the summer when he had been a player here. He had such a feel and love of the game of basketball that I didn't see how he could leave it. So during his final years at GW, I know we were thinking the same thing: *How great a coach he could be.*

I'm very proud of him. I'm very happy for him. And I'm happy because he's worked so hard. He's paid the price. He's left no stone unturned to be the best that he can be. He has done it the right way. He's surrounded himself with good people, which is what you have to do if you're going to be a winner. When he finally left us and went to Duke, as one of Mike Krzyzewski's top assistants, you knew he was on his way to bigger and better things.

Mike came to me and said, "You know the Duke assistant job is open. What do you think?"

I said, "If you want that job, you ought to go after it, and they'll be real lucky if they got you."

And he said, "Will you make the call?"

So I called Coach K, who I knew very well. In fact, when Coach K was in his second or third year there at Duke, he and his wife, Mickie; my wife, Kathy; our five children; and I traveled together to Greece for a clinic. We spent about 10 days over there and so we got to know each other really well. So I called him about Mike, and Coach K named a couple of powerhouse assistants—a couple of unbelievable people in the profession—who had applied for it. And he said, "Well, let me think about it, Morgan." And he called me about 24 hours later and he said, "You know what, I'm going to take your advice. I'm taking Mike Brey."

He'd seen Mike run practices. He'd seen him run drills and got to know him. And so I wasn't surprised that he got the job with Duke. Then he was on his way. From Duke on to Delaware, he was nothing but a winner. From there, he went on to Notre Dame, and the rest is history. But it's history that's being built and developed every day.

I had a definite feeling that when he got the Notre Dame job that it would be his last job because he's so good at what he does. He was going to be so successful at Notre Dame. There was no doubt in my mind he was going to bring in great student-athletes, the type of player who Notre Dame loves to have, and he was going to get the best out of every player he brought in. He knew how to get them to play together. Nobody was going to outcoach him, outwork him, or put more heart into the job than Mike was going to do.

Digger Phelps was a great coach and did a great job at Notre Dame. He had a fabulous record over two decades. So if you surpass his win total, you've really accomplished something. But it's not surprising to me because Mike had such a good understanding of the game that Red Auerbach, the former Boston Celtics coach, praised him for it. He watched some of the games down at the summer league when Mike was coaching the DeMatha teams. And Red told me on two or three occasions, "That kid's good. He's got a real feel of the game. He really understands what's going on. He understands how to get it done."

And Mike's sure proven it. Of course, by going past Digger now, he's just on his way to a more incredible record than ever. Mike now has more than 500 career wins, and when you talk about 500 wins at the collegiate level, that's amazing. There's not a lot of people in front of you. I think it ranks him obviously among the great college coaches in America, and it's just going to keep getting better. It really helped Mike and Notre Dame when they joined the Atlantic Coast Conference. To step into that league, win early, and make the great showing he's made is unbelievable. His journeys to the Elite Eight and winning the ACC Tournament in 2015 show that he's doing something special at a very special university.

When you play for Mike, you know it's not all about winning basketball games. It's about winning the game of life. With Mike, it's the process. He wants to see his players come out as complete people, complete human beings, and good students. Using the old adage, Mike would never let his players fall into the trap of letting basketball use them. He makes sure that they use basketball and all of their skills to be even better at the game of life. And he would be like another Notre Dame coach of yesteryear, Knute Rockne. When they used to ask him what kind of year he expected to have, Rockne would say, "Come back in about 15 years, and when I find out how well they did in the game of life, I'll tell you what kind of year I had." That's the way Mike Brey thinks.

By the time Mike's finished, I see him ranked right up among the very, very best. It's been my honor to coach for a long time, and I think of the great coaches that I have had the honor of knowing and coaching with. I think of John Wooden, Dean Smith, Mike Krzyzewski, Roy Williams, Bob Knight, and on and on. You can see Mike sliding right into that category; there's no doubt in my mind that's where he'll be.

Mike knows that to be a winner you've got to surround yourself with really good people. By adding his former players to his staff, he's sending the message that: if you're a really good person, you've got a chance to be part of this. And once he brings them aboard, they know they've gotten the ultimate compliment. Their coach, their teacher, their friend, their mentor thinks they're something special, and he wants them to be part of the action.

Even with what he's done at Notre Dame on the basketball side, he's so humble. He still gets tickets for kids who are waiting in line. He buys pizzas for kids he sees waiting outside. He really remembers his roots, no doubt about that.

My message for Mike would be: just keep being Mike Brey, just keep being the person you are. Having had the honor of seeing him since he was about nine years old, I know he's somebody really special. And I'll say this about Mike. He's done it very well.

—*Morgan Wootten*
DeMatha Catholic High School head basketball coach
1956–57 to 2001–02
1,274–192 career record

Appendix I: Mike Brey's Wins Against Ranked Opponents

2000–01		Opp	ND	
11–25 vs. Cincinnati		16	14	W 69–51
1–23 vs. Syracuse		11	NR	W 74–60
1–27 @ Georgetown		10	NR	W 78–71
2–21 vs. Boston College		10	18	W 76–75

2001–02		Opp	ND	
1–12 @ Pittsburgh		23	NR	W 56–53
1–30 vs. Pittsburgh		21	NR	W 89–76
2–23 @ Miami		17	NR	W 90–77

2002–03		Opp	ND	
12–2 vs. Marquette		13	NR	W 92–71
12–7 vs. Maryland $		9	NR	W 79–67
12–8 vs. Texas $		2	NR	W 98–92

| 2–9 vs. Pittsburgh | 4 | 10 | W 66–64 |
| 3–22 vs. Illinois * | 11 | 22 | W 68–60 |

2003–04	Opp	ND	
2–9 vs. Connecticut	5	NR	W 80–74

2004–05	Opp	ND	
1–30 vs. Connecticut	19	NR	W 78–74
2–8 vs. Boston College	4	NR	W 68–65

2005–06	Opp	ND	
12–7 @ Alabama	22	NR	W 78–71

2006–07	Opp	ND	
12–3 vs. Maryland (Washington, D.C.)	23	NR	W 81–74
12–7 vs. Alabama	4	NR	W 99–85
1–9 vs. West Virginia	21	t22	W 61–58
2–24 vs. Marquette	16	NR	W 85–73

2007–08	Opp	ND	
1–26 @ Villanova	18	NR	W 90–80
2–9 vs. Marquette	16	22	W 86–83

2008–09	Opp	ND	
11–25 vs. Texas #	6	8	W 81–80
1–5 vs. Georgetown	9	13	W 73–67
2–12 vs. Louisville	5	NR	W 90–57

2009–10	Opp	ND	
1–9 vs. West Virginia	8	NR	W 70–68
2–24 vs. Pittsburgh	12	NR	W 68–53
2–27 vs. Georgetown	11	NR	W 78–64
3–11 vs. Pittsburgh ^	16	NR	W 50–45

2010–11	**Opp**	**ND**	
12–29 vs. Georgetown	9	15	W 69–55
1–4 vs. Connecticut	8	14	W 73–70
1–19 vs. Cincinnati	25	16	W 66–58
1–24 @ Pittsburgh	2	15	W 56–51
2–9 vs. Louisville	16	8	W 89–79 (OT)
2–28 vs. Villanova	19	8	W 93–72
3–5 @ Connecticut	16	8	W 70–67
3–10 vs. Cincinnati ^	25	4	W 89–51

2011–12	**Opp**	**ND**	
12–27 vs. Pittsburgh	22	NR	W 72–59
1–7 @ Louisville	11	NR	W 67–65 (2 OT)
1–21 vs. Syracuse	1	NR	W 67–58
1–29 @ Connecticut	24	NR	W 50–48
2–4 vs. Marquette	15	NR	W 76–59

2012–13	**Opp**	**ND**	
11–29 vs. Kentucky %	8	NR	W 64–50
1–7 @ Cincinnati	21	17	W 66–60
2–9 vs. Louisville	11	25	W 104–101 (5 OT)
2–18 @ Pittsburgh	20	25	W 51–42
3–14 vs. Marquette ^	12	24	W 73–65

2013–14	**Opp**	**ND**	
1–4 vs. Duke	7	NR	W 79–77

2014–15	**Opp**	**ND**	
12–3 vs. Michigan State +	19	NR	W 79–78 (OT)
1–5 @ North Carolina	18	13	W 71–70
1–28 vs. Duke	4	8	W 77–73

3–4 @ Louisville	16	12	W 71–59
3–13 vs. Duke &	2	11	W 74–64
3–14 vs. North Carolina &	19	11	W 90–82
3–21 vs. Butler *	24	8	W 67–64
3–26 vs. Wichita State *	14	8	W 81–70

2015–16	**Opp**	**ND**	
1–16 @ Duke	9	NR	W 95–91
2–6 vs. North Carolina	2	NR	W 80–76
2–13 vs. Louisville	13	NR	W 71–66
3–10 vs. Duke &	19	NR	W 84–79 (OT)

2016–17	**Opp**	**ND**	
1–4 vs. Louisville	9	23	W 77–70
2–11 vs. Florida State	10	NR	W 84–72
3–9 vs. Virginia &	21	22	W 71–58
3–10 vs. Florida State &	16	22	W 77–73

2017–18	**Opp**	**ND**	
11–22 vs. Wichita State #	6	13	W 67–66

*	NCAA Championship	%	SEC/BIG EAST Invitational
#	Maui Invitational	$	BB&T Classic
^	Big East Championship	+	ACC/Big Ten Challenge
&	ACC Championship		

65 wins: 34 at Joyce Center/Purcell Pavilion, 14 on road, 17 at neutral sites

24 vs. Top 10: 1 vs. No. 1, 4 vs. No. 2, 4 vs. No. 4, 2 vs. No. 5, 2 vs. No. 6, 1 vs. No. 7, 3 vs. No. 8, 5 vs. No. 9, 3 vs. No. 10

8 vs. Pittsburgh (4 home, 3 road, 1 Big East Tournament)

7 vs. Louisville (5 home, 2 road)

5 vs. Connecticut (3 home, 2 road)

5 vs. Duke (2 home, 1 road, 2 ACC Tournament)

5 vs. Marquette (4 home, 1 Big East Tournament)

4 vs. Cincinnati (1 home, 1 road, 1 in Indianapolis, 1 Big East Tournament)

4 vs. Georgetown (3 home, 1 road)

3 vs. North Carolina (1 home, 1 road, 1 ACC Tournament)

2 vs. Alabama (1 home, 1 road)

2 vs. Boston College (2 home)

2 vs. Florida State (1 home, 1 ACC Tournament)

2 vs. Maryland (1 in Washington, D.C., 1 BB&T Classic)

2 vs. Syracuse (2 home)

2 vs. Texas (1 Maui Invitational, 1 BB&T Classic)

2 vs. Villanova (1 home, 1 road)

2 vs. West Virginia (2 home)

2 vs. Wichita State (1 Maui Invitational, 1 NCAA Tournament)

Appendix II: Coaching Record

Assistant Coach, DeMatha Catholic High School

1982–83	DeMatha	27–4	Washington Catholic Athletic Conference champion
1983–84	DeMatha	29–2	Washington Catholic Athletic Conference champion
1984–85	DeMatha	31–3	Washington Catholic Athletic Conference champion
1985–86	DeMatha	26–7	—
1986–87	DeMatha	28–6	Washington Catholic Athletic Conference champion

DeMatha record (5 seasons): 139–22 (.863)

Assistant Coach, Duke University

1987–88	Duke	28–7	9–5 ACC	NCAA Final Four
1988–89	Duke	28–8	9–5 ACC	NCAA Final Four
1989–90	Duke	29–9	9–5 ACC	NCAA finalist
1990–91	Duke	32–7	11–3 ACC	NCAA champion
1991–92	Duke	34–2	14–2 ACC	NCAA champion
1992–93	Duke	24–8	10–6 ACC	NCAA second round

282 • Keeping It Loose

| 1993–94 | Duke | 28–6 | 12–4 ACC | NCAA finalist |
| 1994–95 | Duke | 13–18 | 2–14 ACC | — |

Duke record (8 seasons): 216–65 (.768)

Head Coach, University of Delaware

1995–96	Delaware	15–12	11–7 NAC	—
1996–97	Delaware	15–16	8–10 AE	—
1997–98	Delaware	20–10	12–6 AE	NCAA first round
1998–99	Delaware	25–6	15–3 AE	NCAA first round
1999–00	Delaware	24–8	14–4 AE	NIT first round

Delaware record (5 seasons) as head coach: 99–52 (.656)

Head Coach, University of Notre Dame

2000–01	Notre Dame	20–10	11–5 Big East	NCAA second round
2001–02	Notre Dame	22–11	10–6 Big East	NCAA second round
2002–03	Notre Dame	24–10	10–6 Big East	NCAA Regional semifinalist
2003–04	Notre Dame	19–13	9–7 Big East	NIT third round
2004–05	Notre Dame	17–12	9–7 Big East	NIT first round
2005–06	Notre Dame	16–14	6–10 Big East	NIT second round
2006–07	Notre Dame	24–8	11–5 Big East	NCAA first round

Big East Conference Coach of the Year

| 2007–08 | Notre Dame | 25–8 | 14–4 Big East | NCAA second round |

Big East Conference Coach of the Year

| 2008–09 | Notre Dame | 21–15 | 8–10 Big East | NIT semifinalist |
| 2009–10 | Notre Dame | 23–12 | 10–8 Big East | NCAA first round |

2010–11	Notre Dame	27–7	14–4 Big East	NCAA second round

AP National Coach of the Year, Big East Conference Coach of the Year

2011–12	Notre Dame	22–12	13–5 Big East	NCAA first round
2012–13	Notre Dame	25–10	11–7 Big East	NCAA first found
2013–14	Notre Dame	15–17	6–12 ACC	–––
2014–15	Notre Dame	32–6	14–4 ACC	NCAA Regional finalist
2015–16	Notre Dame	24–12	11–7 ACC	NCAA Regional finalist
2016–17	Notre Dame	26–10	12–6 ACC	NCAA second round
2017–18	Notre Dame	21–15	8–10 ACC	NIT second round

Notre Dame record (18 seasons) as head coach: 403–202 (.666)
Career record (23 seasons) as head coach: 502–254 (.664)

Acknowledgments

THIS STORY COULD NEVER BE TOLD IF NOT FOR THESE INDIVIDUALS:

My parents, who set the perfect examples for me and motivated me to teach and coach.

Tish, Kyle, and Callie Brey. We always talk about the Notre Dame family, and my own family has been such an important part of all that has happened here.

Morgan Wootten and Mike Krzyzewski—I would not be where I am today if not for the interest they showed in me and how their programs set the bar for me. The DeMatha and Duke programs ranked as the gold standard in so many ways, and so the manner in which those two did business became such a big part of me and my own philosophies. I can't thank them enough for showing me the way.

Father Monk Malloy and Father John Jenkins, the two university presidents I've had the privilege of serving under in South Bend. They set the tone for how athletics are done at Notre Dame.

Jack Swarbrick and Kevin White, my two athletic directors and bosses at Notre Dame. They were always here to celebrate the great moments and lend support. They always made sure the compass was pointed in the right direction.

The dozens of players who made the decision to come to Notre Dame, to compete, and to represent our program and our university.

Jim Fraleigh, our current sport administrator, and predecessors Bill Scholl and Jim Phillips—they handled so many administrative areas for us, and that allowed me and my staff to teach and coach.

Sean Kearney, Anthony Solomon, Gene Cross, Lewis Preston, Martin Ingelsby, Rod Balanis, Ryan Humphrey, Ryan Ayers, Harold Swanagan, and Eric Atkins. We had no chance for success without the commitment and dedicated work of the members of my coaching staff.

Skip Meyer (our athletic trainer), Tony Rolinski (our director of strength and conditioning), Pat Holmes (our academic adviser), and Alan Wasielewski and Bernie Cafarelli (media relations)—they all played such key roles in supporting our student-athletes. The entire staff at Fighting Irish Media has helped take our communications to a new level.

Sarah Futa, my administrative assistant who consistently kept the ball rolling on this project. Sarah, Stephanie Reed, and Karen Wesolek all kept me and my schedule on the same page.

Our Notre Dame students and fans, who make Purcell Pavilion night in and night out a fabulous place for our players to show what they can do.

Digger Phelps, who has been so valuable in helping me understand what being the basketball coach at Notre Dame is all about.

Suzanne Eyler, who believed in this project from Day One. Jeff Fedotin, our Triumph Books editor, who always made sure to ask the right questions to ensure these pages read the way we wanted them to read.